# THE DIVINE TRAP

## Background on
## the Parables
## Series A

## Richard Carl Hoefler

THE DIVINE TRAP

ISBN 0-89536-445-X

PRINTED IN U.S.A.

*Dedicated to*

*Ebenezer Lutheran Church*

*Columbia, South Carolina*

*Celebrating the*

*One Hundred and Fiftieth*

*Anniversary*

# CONTENTS

# Introduction

This is the second volume of a two-volume work on the parables used in the Three-Year cycle of the Church Year. This volume deals with the eleven parables from Matthew, Series A of the Unified Lectionary.

Jesus told parables to his people that they might better understand his message and mission. He also told parables to people considered his enemies. Some scholars have called this use of parables "weapons of warfare." But it is better thought of as a surgical use of the parables. The cutting, knife-like edge is still there but its intention is not to destroy and kill but to correct and cure.

Today, the parables are more than likely some of the most popular passages of Scripture. They appeal to people because they are stories, and everybody likes to hear a good story. However, a parable is more than just a good story; it is a metaphor — a figure of speech in which the similiarity of one object or action to another is implied. Metaphor literally means "future talk," and that is what the parables of Jesus are. They are stories meant to open up new visions of reality, new insights into spirituality, and new options for human potentiality.

The parables invite both friends and enemies of Jesus into a story, to become involved in that story, participate in it, and ultimately be changed by it.

The chapters of this book are not sermons, but discussions based on classroom lectures concerned with presenting the preaching values of the parables. Ideas from scholars are presented, together with illustrations and suggestions, in an effort to provide preachers and teachers the material necessary for the construction of sermons and lectures on the parables in Matthew.

A sermon is what happens when a text is brought into contact with life. The Word makes contact with the world and a spark ignites. That spark is the basis for a sermon. For each person this contact point and spark may be different, as the experiences of people are different. And for the same person sparks may occur at different points of contact when situations change. Therefore, this book is designed to create "live ends" of the Word and the world in the hope that as they are brought together in the reader's mind, the needed spark for a sermon will occur.

## Parable Interpretation

For more than a thousand years the parables were interpreted as allegory. Each detail of the story was viewed as a miniature vault wherein spiritual mysteries were stored. In 1910 Juelicher singlehandedly destroyed the allegorical method. He maintained that the intention of the parables was to prove or convince, and since only one thing could be proved at a time, the parable could have only one single point. For Juelicher this was a neat little moral teaching. The popular expression of this approach was given in the definition of a parable as an "earthly example of a heavenly truth."

The most influential work on the parables was done by the historical critics. Cadoux of Glasgow (1931) paved the way for this approach to the parables, but it was C. H. Dodd of Oxford (1935) and his German contemporary Joachim Jeremias (1947) who brought the interpreters of the parables an awareness of the change the parables underwent as they moved from an oral tradition to a written form. They pointed out the decisive difference between **tradition,** what the parables meant when Jesus first used them, and **redaction,** how the Early Church and the writers of the Gospels used the parables in their accounts. The parables were now seen not as neat little moral truths, but as weapons of warfare Jesus used to attack his enemies and as exhortations to the church to adjust to changing conditions. The main concern was to discover the historical setting in which the parables were used.

This historical interpretation dominated the academic world of parable interpretation until about ten years ago when two new approaches were suggested by Narrative Theology and Structural Exegesis.

Narrative Theology and Structural Exegesis are both reactions to the schools of historical criticism. Their intention is not to destroy or detract from the contributions made by the historical critics, but to add another dimension or consideration to the hermeneutical process. As mentioned above, this century has been dominated by the historical method. The problem was to move behind the biblical record to the event itself. The task was to identify within the Scriptures what were the original words of Jesus and what were the additions and changes made by the Early Church.

Redaction Criticism begins with the author and attempts to establish his intentionality. He had a purpose for his writing and this determined the way in which he selected, organized and presented his materials. Literary Criticism went a step further to examine the sources used by the writers to see how they reflected a previous purpose of the Early Church as they adapted the materials of oral tradition to fit their particular situation, such as the delayed coming of Jesus, the influx of Gentiles into the Church, and the moral needs of practicing Christianity in a pagan world. Form Criticism attempted to get back to the original oral tradition and see how the accounts of Our Lord's life and his teachings were used in worship, education, and evangelism.

Now in each case the criterion was history. A research of the materials of Scriptures was done to establish the facts, what Jesus said in the first place, and how these materials were changed and adjusted to fit particular needs. Now Narrative Theology and Structural Exegesis are both reactions against what they consider to be an over-emphasis on the historical. They take the position that in the process of discovering the facts of revelation, the inner meaning of the texts themselves has been slighted. The historical approach has been so concerned with what Jesus actually said and what the Church did with what he said, that it has failed to do justice to the full meaning of what he said. So rather than being concerned with the author or the historical setting and use of the text, Narrative Theology and Structural Exegesis have focused in on the text itself. They view the text as story — as an account which possesses in and of itself an integrity. And as text alone, they have examined it from a literary point of view to discover the meaning which it possesses as a story.

The basic difference between the historical critics and the Narrative-Structural critics is that the historical critics look through the text to something else — namely the setting or situation outside the text. By relating the parable to this outside material which surrounded it, the meaning of the parable could be established. The Narrative-Structural interpreters look at the text itself. The form and the relationship of the various elements within the story determine its meaning or meanings.

In the discussions of the parables which follow, both the interpretation of the historical critics and the Narrative-Structural critics will be used because both enlighten the total impact of the parables. The parables will be viewed, however, primarily as story. But they are stories which can be understood only as related to two other primary stories.

Three stories concern us in the following treatment of parables. First, there is the story of the parable itself. Here the interpretation of Narrative Theology and Structural Exegesis will be of great help. Second, there is the larger story told by the Bible itself in which the parable is imbedded. Here the historical critics will be informative. The third story is the story of the listeners. Each person who hears a parable has a life story of his own. He has had certain experiences which have created problems, established ideas and opinions, and developed habitual reactions. The task of parable interpretation is to place the story of the parable alongside both of the other two stories.

First, the story of the parable is placed alongside the total story of the Bible. The Creation, Fall, Covenant, Law,

Prophets, the life of Jesus and the writings of Paul are seen as the background in which the parables were told. The parables seldom introduce new revelations, but in each case they dramatize an aspect of the total story. It is not necessary that the original teller of the parable was aware of this relationship. For example, in the Parable of the Soils, it is not absolutely necessary that Jesus had the optimism of God in mind when he told the parable. If, when the parable is placed over against the total revelation of Scripture, the interpreter sees this biblically revealed optimism of God dramatized in the story the parable tells, then it is legitimate if the spark for the sermon occurs at this point. The parable as story is a dynamic Word of God, and if, when placed in contact with the Bible story, a spark occurs and a relationship is seen, this can be an acceptable basis for a sermon.

In the same manner, when you place the story of the parable alongside the life stories of the listeners, certain relationships will emerge. They may not have been in the mind of the original teller of the story, but they are legitimate if the parable honestly speaks to this experience in the life of the listener.

The parables as story have an integrity in and of themselves. As most scholars agree, they represent some of the most original and reliable materials of the Gospels. Here, more than anywhere else in the New Testament, we have words actually spoken by Jesus. The parables are not therefore secondary materials which simply illustrate the Bible story, but are a vital part of that revelation. As the Word of God, they are dynamic and not static. They are not nuts which have to be cracked to find within them the static truth previously placed there by Jesus. With the rest of Scripture, they are living words spoken by God and when brought into contact with the listeners can convey ever fresh understandings of God's will for us today.

Some readers may feel that the method suggested by focusing on the comparative relationship of the three stories is a return to a form of allegorization. This is not the case, however. Allegorization is finding within each detail of the story a hidden, comparative relationship. Each character and object has its corresponding reality in life. The method in this discussion of the parables is that of "plot parallelism." The parables are viewed basically as dramas in which the action in most cases is more important than the characters or the object involved. The parables are stories in which the similarity of one action to another action is implied. We see in the plot of the parable a dramatization of actions within the story of the Bible and within our own experiences.

The important thing, therefore, is not that the parables are stories with one point, but that they are stories with a plot. It is the plot of the parable that is the key to interpretation. When this plot is placed alongside the story of the Bible and the story of our lives, the meaning and the message of the parables emerge for our time.

*1*

# A Life-Endurance Policy

**The Parable of the Two House Builders**
**Matthew 7:24-29**

Once there were three little pigs. Each built a house. The wolf came and blew the houses away, except for one. Now Jesus tells a similar story about two men. Each builds a house. The storms come and only one house stands.

Jesus told many stories about farming and the problems that happen in the market place. Now it would seem that the carpenter's son from Nazareth is on more familiar ground as he tells about two men who build a house. The dramatic climax comes with the storm. The foolish man sees his house fall. The wise man's house stands and endures the storm.

The key to understanding this parable will be found when we can answer the question, "Why did the foolish man's house fall, and why did the wise man's house stand?" To begin this search for the answer, we need to see that when a man decides to build a house, he first selects the design, size, and style of the house he wants to build, then he selects the materials and the workmanship that will go into it, and finally the site where he will build his house.

## Construction

Most interpreters of this parable focus in on "construction." They follow Luke's version of the parable where he points out that the flood came but "could not shake it (the house) because it had been well built." (Luke 6:48) This would follow the story of "Three Little Pigs" where one built his house of straw, the second built his house of sticks, and the third little pig built with bricks. When the wolf came and tried to blow the houses down, only the third little pig's house stood because it was built with bricks. So in the parable the wise man's house withstood the storm and flood because the construction was sound.

The rabbis at the time of our Lord were telling a similar story.[1] They said that a man who does good works and knows the Torah is like a man who builds his house with a stone foundation underneath, and a brick and clay construction above. When the floods come they cannot wash the house away. The man who does not do good works and who fails to learn the Torah is like the house builder who makes his foundation of bricks and clay and builds his house of stones. The clay mortar cannot withstand the waters of the flood and the house falls.

It is quite apparent that the point of the rabbis' story is the construction of the house. A foundation of clay and bricks melts away in the storm. But the stone foundation holds. It would seem that Luke was influenced by this rabbinic tale when he recorded our Lord's parable of the two builders.

Now we know that Jesus used many of the current rabbinic stories of his day as the basis of his own parables. But in most cases, he would change the original story, and the change he made was decisive to understand the new teachings he was proclaiming. Therefore, the account of Matthew which changes the focal point of the traditional rabbinic story is much more suggestive.

## The Choice of Site

Matthew's version of the parable recognizes the subtle change made in the traditional story of the two builders and stresses it. According to Matthew's account, "But it did not fall because it had been built on the rock." The assumption can be made that both houses were well built. The vital difference was not construction but choice of site. The foolish man built his house on sand. The wise man built his house on **the** rock.

I remember when I was young and my family was out for a Sunday afternoon drive. We would often comment on the houses along the way. We would point out the most beautiful and impressive homes. But my father would frequently interrupt and say that the house was fine but he would never own it in that location. He would point out that all the other properties around it drained into that lot. Every time there was a heavy rain that house would end up with water in the basement. My father had learned from experience what never entered our minds, the fact that site and location are essential considerations when judging the suitability of a house.

This is really the point of the parable as Matthew records it. The issue is not so much a matter of sound construction but of the site, the location chosen to build the house.

## The Setting of the Parable

Now accepting this as the main thrust of the parable, what lesson was Jesus teaching with such a story? Here we need to turn our attention to the setting of the parable in the total accounts of Matthew and Luke. Both place the Parable of the Two Builders immediately after the Sermon on the Mount (or the Plain, as Luke would have it). Jesus had just finished presenting his basic teachings concerning the Kingdom of God. Both Matthew and Luke introduce the parable with the statement, "Everyone then who hears these words of mine and does them will be like . . ." The setting would therefore suggest that the parable has to do with our response to the words — the teachings of Jesus.

The temptation is to stop here and focus attention on the contrast between hearing and doing. Faced with the pressing need of a sermon for next Sunday, the contrast between just hearing the words of our Lord and actually carrying them out in our lives suggests a great opportunity to denounce the indifference and laziness we see in our congregations. We decide to preach a sermon on the virtues of hard work and honest labor, and advise our listeners to build their lives well.

However, to follow this approach is actually to miss the main point of the parable. For in the story that Jesus tells, both men build. The Parable of the Two Builders is not about one man who built well and another man who was lazy and just threw his house together any old way. Both men engaged in the hard work of building a house. The point of the parable is that one man wasted all his hard work because he built his house on the wrong site.

### My Words

Christ came to a people who were quite active in their faith. For the most part his audience was made up of people who were in the process of building their lives — and building them well — on the Torah and the teachings of those who knew the Law and expounded it. Jesus is saying to the Jews with this parable, "You are doing a good job of building, but your site and location are all wrong. You are building on the Torah and the Law. I have come to give you a new site, a new location to build your lives." Christ had come with a new option for life building. He came presenting a new teaching. He came to establish a new covenant between man and God. And that new option, new teaching, new covenant, was **Himself** and the message he brought.

The most important phrase in the statement Jesus makes as he introduces this parable is, "these words of **mine**." It is not enough to hear and do, but to hear **his** words, and act on

**his** words. One greater than the Law and Moses had come. Christ places **himself** over against all that people held most important for their lives. It is his words and his words alone that are the only building site for the life that will endure.

Matthew apparently understood this, for after this parable he adds the statement, "And when Jesus finished these sayings, the crowd were astonished at his teachings, for he taught as one who had authority, and not as their scribes." (Matthew 7:28-29) The fact that action should follow hearing is not new and astonishing to the Jews or to us. But the blunt, direct assumption that Christ, and Christ's words alone are the only secure basis for life was a shocking and radical claim for the Jews and perhaps for some of us. There is no room here for compromise or polite arbitration. Christ has placed himself in a position that challenges and threatens all other authorities. One greater than the Law and Moses had come. Is it any wonder that his life ended on a cross? For here is no nice little teacher wisely proclaiming an acceptable and traditional morality, or a brilliant young rabbi interpreting the Law. Here is a radical revolutionary, who is either a fool or God.

### In Christ the Kingdom of God Has Come

During the Second World War a test pilot was flying over the Gulf of Mexico. His aircraft developed trouble and he was forced to bail out. Landing safely in the water, he freed himself from his parachute and started swimming toward the land. The shore looked miles away from him. The longer he swam, the farther away the shore appeared to be. Finally, he was exhausted. This was it. Slowly he resigned himself to his watery death. He relaxed and let his body lower into the water. Suddenly, to his utter amazement, his feet hit bottom. The sand bars of the gulf extend far out into the bay, and he was in water that was just shoulder deep. He had been struggling and swimming for his very life in water that was not over his head.

Christ was speaking to people who believed that the kingdom of God was in the distance. They were desperately struggling toward the promise of that which was yet to come. The message Christ proclaimed was that their salvation was not in the distance ahead of them, but with them now. Standing in their midst was the fulfillment of the promises. He — the Son of God — spoke, and as he spoke he placed beneath them the ground rock of eternity. **Hear me and my words. Plant your feet firmly on my teachings and you will build a life that will endure.**

So the issue of the parable is not "doing." The flyer in our story did something. In fact, he did all he possibly could do to the point of exhaustion. But his doing was useless, because his vision was all wrong. He was looking to the distant shore, and building his hopes on the land ahead, when in reality the solid ground of his salvation was beneath him within his reach. Christ says with this parable, "So then, everyone who hears **these words of mine** and obeys them will be like a wise man who built his house on the rock." And there is no other rock but Christ and his words.

### The Storm and the Flood

This leads us to the dramatic center of the parable — the storm and the flood. We have said that the two men in the parable built well. Under normal circumstances there was nothing wrong with the construction of their houses. But life is not all sunny and peaceful. There are storms, moments of crisis, and disaster. What then? The parable points out that in times of such testing, no matter how well the house is built, it is the site that counts and makes the decisive difference.

This parable is not about construction and materials used to build; it is about what happens in the crisis of a storm. It is about what enables a structure to endure and stand against the storm. In the story of the Three Little Pigs, each had a very comfortable little house until the wolf came. So the parable of our Lord is about what happens when the wolf comes to the door. It is a parable of emergency. It is a parable of the urgency to prepare for the unexpected. The parable says to us, "Build on the best and prepare for the worst."

## Life Endurance

Now most of us are aware of the necessity of preparing for the unexpected — the sudden storms that are a part of life. Accidents, fire and wind, robbery and death are why we invest in "a Piece of the Rock with Prudential," and place ourselves in the "Mighty Hands of Allstate." And then that big dent in our paycheck called "Withholding" constantly reminds us of the cost and the importance of preparing for the future. But Jesus is not talking about financial security — as important as that is. Rather, he is talking about the damage the storms of life do to us personally. He is talking about discouragement, despair, frustration and fear. He is talking about the loss of meaning and purpose, even the loss of life itself.

It is interesting that what we commonly call "Life Insurance" really isn't life insurance at all. It is **death** insurance. It is to protect us against the financial problems caused by death. Jesus, on the other hand, is talking about **life** insurance. Or perhaps better stated to avoid confusion, Jesus is talking about life **endurance**. How can we endure the storms of life, and that particularly destructive storm called death? Christ says to us, "Build your life on me and my words, and you will be able to endure every storm."

## Endurance in an Impartial World

One of the most frustrating problems of our faith is that we live in a world that is so impartial. Tragedy strikes both good and bad with equal frequency and force.

A tornado will skip over a junkyard and level to the ground a school next door. Cancer kills the creative artist and the productive scientist at the height of their careers. An insane criminal lives and a president dies. And we want to cry out, "Where is the justice of it all? Is there no order? Is there no concern for value in God's creation? Where is the personal will of an all-loving God in this impartial world of fickle fate?"

## Avoid or Endure

There seem to be just two ways to look at disaster in the world, and most of us settle for the most obvious. The most obvious approach is to avoid disaster at all costs. This is the attitude of the cautious man. He believes that by doing only that which is right he can avoid disaster. He reasons that in a just and orderly world a man who does right and works hard should have an advantage over an evil and lazy man. But we know from experience that this just isn't so. It seems so right, yet it is wrong.

The other approach toward disaster is that of the courageous man. His main concern is not how to avoid but how to endure disaster. He gets much more out of life, because he is not afraid of life.

Now the point of the Parable of the Two Builders is directed to the courageous attitude toward life. The storm comes to both houses. This cannot be avoided. Therefore, don't be afraid to build, but courageously build on a foundation that will enable you to endure the storms.

## The World Is Impartial but God Is not Indifferent

The wisdom and foolishness of people have little effect upon the weather, because as we have pointed out, we live in an impartial world. But does this mean God is impartial in his personal relationships with his people? The parable says, "No." True, the storms come to the good as well as the bad, the wise as well as the foolish. But even though the world God has created is impartial, God is not indifferent. God is concerned. He stands ready and willing to give the strength and the power needed to endure the disasters of an impartial world. That is why he revealed himself in Jesus Christ. That is why God did not remain aloof and silent. That is why he gave humanity the promise. And that is why his promise became incarnate in the person of Jesus Christ. As Christ speaks, God speaks, and his words become for us a place where we might take a stand and build our lives and endure.

Our relationship to God does make a difference — a crucial difference. The house built on a rock represents that difference. God enables the righteous to endure the disasters life impartially hurls in our path. God gives not special privileges to the righteous but special power.

### Absorbant Power

Now this special power God gives could be called the power of endurance, but it is better called **absorbant power**. It is the power not only to endure the storms of tragedy, but actually to overcome them.

I once knew a man who would display his great strength by challenging children to hit him as hard as they could in the stomach. They would tear into him with all their youthful enthusiasm and energy. They would hit him with all they had until they fell exhausted at his feet. He remained unaffected. That is the power God gives. The power to stand up and take it. And when disasters and troubles of life have done their best, or worst, the righteous still stands. For his strength is the strength of the rock on which he stands.

This is the power of the gigantic oak that bends with the winds of the storm, and when the storm has blown itself out, the oak still stands.

When Christ went willingly to the cross, he stood up to the final enemy of us all — death. He accepted all the suffering and pain evil could muster. God the Father directed Christ into that satanic storm because God in his infinite wisdom knew that ultimate power is not expressed in the avoidance of conflict, but in a direct engagement and encounter with it. Therefore, Christ opened himself to the cross. He submitted his innocent body to the full blast of the storm and drew into his nakedness the total flood of evil, thereby transforming it, changing it, rendering it useless and helpless. Because this Son of God was our Savior, that same power is ours. As we surrender ourselves to him and let down the full weight of ourselves on the rock of his power, and build our new life that results on this site, we will stand despite all the storms.

The moralists look at this Parable of the Two Builders and see only the theology of the Three Little Pigs, that we should strive to build the houses of our lives well so that the storms will not destroy them. The wise person looks at this parable through the cross and sees Christ giving us the power to endure the storms of life. Christ says, "Hear these words of mine. They possess within themselves not only the power to do but to endure. Trust not in your own wisdom or strength to build, but build on me, and I will give you all you need."

# 2

# The Divine Optimism of God

**The Parable of the Sower**
**Matthew 13:1-9**

Today a violent revolution that attempts to radically change society is associated with the Communists. In the days of our Lord it was the social doctrine of the Apocalypticists. They believed that one day soon God would forcefully break into this world and establish his kingdom with brutal power. He would purge the world of wickedness and destroy all evil.

Our text begins with Jesus at the height of his popularity. The apocalyptic expectation of a violent revolution was the current issue of the day. The common people were convinced that this Jesus of Nazareth, son of a carpenter, was the promised apocalyptic hero. Everywhere he went, crowds followed him. On this day there was such a great crowd about him, pushing and shoving him, that he was forced to get into a boat and push out from the shore in order to speak with them.

Expectations were running high. There was excitement in the air. In the minds of the people who gathered that day to hear Jesus, the hour had come for ringing the bells of rebellion and freedom.

Against this apocalyptic background and potentially

explosive situation, Jesus began his message with the fantastic phrase, "A sower went forth to sow." It was a far cry from the battle slogan the people had expected, but therein is the shocking uniqueness of this parable-teller and the stories he told. The Kingdom he was proclaiming was not an explosive day of doom and destruction. It was a seed growing silently in a field of responsive soil.

We cannot be absolutely certain how the people reacted that day to what Jesus said. Undoubtedly they were bitterly disappointed, or at least stunned and confused. More than likely many of them were completely disillusioned with this new prophet, and started from that moment on to look elsewhere for their apocalyptic leader.

Matthew would seem to imply confusion as the mood of the occasion, for he follows this Parable of the Sower with a discussion among the disciples concerning the use of parables as a teaching technique. "Why do you use parables when you talk with them?" the disciples asked. Jesus answered by quoting from the prophecy of Isaiah where the people expected one thing while God was desiring something else. The people of this prophecy were described as dull of mind, with deaf ears, and blind eyes.

"You are fortunate," Jesus says to his disciples, "for your eyes see and your ears hear." Or in other words, Jesus tells the disciples not to be like the crowd who has its mind already made up as to the nature of the Kingdom of God. **Keep an open mind. Listen to me and you will hear the truth. The Kingdom of God comes not in violent revolution. No, the coming of the Kingdom is like a sower going forth to plant his fields.**

Here then is where we must begin to find the meaning of this parable. It stands as a part of our Lord's unique message concerning the nature of the Kingdom of God. To the surprise of all, Jesus proclaims that God comes not as a warrior, but as a farmer. He comes not with a sword but with a seed. He comes not to lead an army of angry men, but to cultivate a field of rich, responsive soil. He comes not to destroy the land, but to plant and eventually harvest an abundant crop from the land.

## An Easy Parable

Today the Parable of the Sower is not so shocking or revolutionary as when our Lord first told it. In fact, it is more than likely one of the most popular of all the parables Jesus told. Give a beginning class in sermon preparation an assignment to preach on any parable they choose, and you can be certain that several will select the Parable of the Sower.

It may be that a sermon outline seems so ready-made in the four types of soil; or it may be the fact of having the exegesis and explanation conveniently tacked on to the end of the parable. Whatever the reason, the danger is that what makes the parable attractively simple and instantly perceptible may prove to be only a pitfall that actually prohibits one from discovering its real message.

## Diversity

Diversity of interpretation dominates any review of how scholars have treated this parable in the past. For example, the question of authenticity of the explanation following the parable is a cause of much controversy. On the one hand you have Jeremias[1] who believes the explanation to be an addition of the early church. On the other, you have C.F.D. Moule[2] who accepts it as an authentic interpretation of Jesus himself.

Diversity is also evidenced in the variety of focal points found in the parable by different interpreters. Some are attracted to the sower, others to the seed, and still others to the four soils. Some scholars, following the rule of "end stress," zero in on the great harvest at the close of the story. As we shall see, even the field can be singled out for special attention.

All of these approaches can prove fruitful to any complete

understanding of the parable. It is a good story, and like any good story it can say many things depending on who tells it and who hears it.

## The Sower

The story is an account of what normally happened when a sower in Jesus' day went forth to sow his seeds. Some take the position that Jesus saw an actual sower in the field and was inspired to tell the parable with that particular sower in mind. But the use of the generic article, **ho speiron** ("the sower"), indicates the sower as a class. Others suggest that Jesus was appealing to a symbol of God as the sower which was well established in the Jewish mind. The "Great Sower" was the familiar metaphor for God used in the Old Testament (Isaiah 55:10, Jeremiah 31:27, Ezekiel 36:9, Hosea 2:23, Zechariah 10:9).

If Jesus had in mind that the sower was God, this would tend to place the image of the sower as a vital and an important element in the parable. Eta Linnemann disagrees with this. She points out that even though the parable mentions the sower first, he does not stand at the center of the story.[3]

Many interpreters, on the other hand, find great significance in the actions of the sower. The sower may not be God, but the actions of the sower tell us something about the actions of God. For example, we see here the incredible optimism of God.

## The Optimism of God

Despite the fact that the bad soils outnumber the good soil three to one, there is an undergirding optimism permeating the parable. It begins with a sower scattering his seeds into the most unlikely places. He is neither cautious nor calculating about what he does. The parable suggests he sows with a kind of sprightly abandonment, "and some fell among the wayside, and some on the rock, and some among the thorns."

The bad odds against a good harvest and the careless sowing, however, do not ruin the chance of a good crop. The parable ends with an abundant harvest. The usual expectation would be a tenfold yield. Here it is a hundredfold — ten times greater than would normally be expected.

Now the carelessness of the sowing and the great harvest both connote the optimism of God. Many scholars support this view by quoting the fifty-fifth chapter of Isaiah, "So shall my word that goes forth from my mouth; it shall not return to me empty, but it shall accomplish that which I purpose, and prosper in the thing for which I sent it." God is optimistic because he knows that his efforts, no matter how free, cannot fail. He can afford to be careless with his seed, for he knows that even a little can accomplish great things and produce a mighty harvest.

It is often difficult for us to comprehend this type of carelessness on God's part. We take ourselves and our work with such great seriousness. We are afraid of risk. We tend not to invest or spend our money unless it is a sure and certain thing. We look with a cautious and calculating eye hungering for measurable returns for all of our spending. We carefully weigh each situation and worry constantly that we have made a mistake and invested foolishly. God, however, is no worrier. God is confident in his carelessness. He knows that despite the lack of ready response and immediate results, the harvest will surely come, and it will be a bumper crop.

We should rejoice in this characteristic of God, for without such careless confidence, without this divine optimism, there would be no prophets, no Christ, no Bible, no church, and certainly no mercy for the undeserving — and therefore no offer of forgiveness and love in your direction or mine.

## The Soils

Biblical scholars have dug around in these four soils for years trying to find their hidden treasures. Preachers have literally worked the soil to death relishing the opportunity the three bad soils present to vent their spleen on the difficult people we are called to serve. The three bad soils are easily identified among the undesirable characters quite familiar to us all.

## The Path

The beaten path is the tough customer who has never responded and who never will. His heart is paved with the concrete of conceit. His soul is solidified with stubborn self-centeredness. No matter what his astrological sign, his horoscope is always the same: make no new commitments, maintain the status quo, and avoid all change.

## The Rocky Ground

The rocky ground is the shallow enthusiast who gushes all over the place at every new venture that comes along, but as soon as you hit the long hard pull he fades away never to be heard of again until the job is over. For him it is "easy come, easy go."

Like the little boy who was always falling out of bed, he said of himself, "I guess I go to sleep too close to where I got in." So the rocky ground character is quick to act, but equally quick to fall asleep. He says it is due to the fact that he has a clear conscience. But the truth is he goes to sleep easily because he has no conscience at all.

He is an easy convert on the first ballot. You will find him dashing down the sawdust trail when the emotions are high and there's a fever pitch of excitement in the air. But the morning after when the time comes to put convictions into action he's nowhere to be found.

## The Thorny Soil

The thorny soil is the popular and successful guy. Everybody likes him, but no one really knows him. He is always too busy to sit down and talk. He is always pointed out as the hot prospect for the church. The only trouble is that he's a hot prospect for everything that comes down the road. He is an habitual joiner. Everything takes root and grows in his mind. His life is a virtual jungle.

He is really not a bad guy, he is just too busy with second-rate, thorn-like things. He is good but he is good for nothing. What this character needs is not so much to be converted, as to be cultivated. He needs to have his life pruned, his time organized, his interests controlled so that he can settle in on one thing and get it done. But he never does because he is so busy talking to someone else while he is being given sound advice.

So the three bad soils stand as rather grim possibilities for the task of planting a promising crop. What the birds miss will be scorched by the barren rock, or will be choked to death by thorny competitors. However, there is yet the good soil to be considered, and we will have more to say about that later.

## Various Ways of Hearing

Some interpreters find that the image of the soils suggests not four different people but four ways each of us hears the word of God.

A. M. Hunter,[4] for example, points out that the footpath is listening to God's words with our ears only. It represents the "in one ear, out the other" type of hearing.

The shallow soil is when we listen with our minds only. While we are in the act of listening, we are attentive and apparently interested. We might even be moved to the edge of persuasion. But we soon forget what we heard. We are quickly bored and turn to fresher and newer ideas.

The thorns are representative of listening with our emotions only. We are easily moved by the prevailing mood. But the morning after, in the cold light of dawn, when we have had time to think about it and consider the shape of our bank account and the mountain of bills to be paid, we decide the practical thing is to deal with the issues at home first.

The good soil, according to Hunter, is listening to the Word of God with our whole being. We think it through, feel it, are moved by it. We surrender our whole self to God and go out into the world to save him.

So the four soils may be four different characters and how they react in their own typical fashion. Or they may be four different ways in which we hear the Word at one time or another.

## A Good View of Bad Soils

Thielicke comes to this same conclusion by a very unique approach.[5] He starts out with a positive view of the bad soils. He points out that the path was never intended to receive seeds. Its function is to enable people to find a safe way to walk. For this end it was created, and we should not judge or condemn a path for failing to be good field soil. The path may be bad soil for planting, but it is perfectly good soil for walking.

The rocky ground may be bad soil for seeds. But it, too, was never intended for farming. In our previous parable we concluded that rock was a good foundation on which to build a house that could withstand the storms. So rocky soil is bad for seed planting, but is good for house building.

The thorny ground also has its function. In the times of Jesus, thorns were an essential source of fuel, particularly for cooking. Thorny ground is bad for raising wheat, but it is good when you need a fire in the stove to bake bread.

We cannot blame the soils for being what they are. They are in their own way contributing a worthwhile service. Where would we be without paths to walk on, and rocks to build with, or thorns to burn?

Thielicke goes on from these observations to say that we should not interpret the four soils as four different types of people, for each person would be predestined by the type of soil he is. Rather, the truth of the parable according to Thielicke is that each person has all four soils within him. There are times when we are hard, or rocky or thorny soil. But there are other times when we are receptive and fertile for the Word.

## Moments of Sensitivity

This is particularly important in the areas of evangelism and witnessing. We who are called to be sowers and speak God's Word should realize that in the lives of people there are moments of special sensitivity — moments when they are right for the hearing of the Word.

When our Lord says that we should be fishers of men, he is not talking about the enthusiastic week-end fisherman who fishes for the pleasure of it. He is talking about the skilled fisherman whose very life existence depends on knowing how and where and when to cast in the net and bring home to a waiting village a life-sustaining catch.

Even the week-end fisherman knows that you don't just walk up to any stream, throw in your hook, and catch a fish. You have to be at the right place at the right time, with the right bait. So with witnessing it is a matter of timing and knowing people.

Johnny picks up his baseball glove and heads for the door. Mother suddenly remembers that the pastor last Sunday in his sermon encouraged parents to sit down and talk to their children about God. So she catches Johnny on the run, sits him down and says, "We are going to take a few minutes and talk about God."

Nothing results. The timing is off. Johnny at that moment is hard soil. His mind is a beaten path directed exclusively in the direction of the baseball field. Any seedling word about

God and religion at that moment is for the birds.

On the other hand, there will be moments — good moments — when Johnny is receptive soil. Perhaps that time when his dog was run over and killed by a passing car, and he came in and asked his mother why things have to die. One word spoken to his tearful question, at that moment, is worth a hundred lectures about God either at home or in the church.

The man who stops people on the street and demands to know if they have been saved may be sincere and well-intentioned, but in many cases he does more harm than good. He actually creates hard and thorny ground for the future sowing of the seed by his bad timing. Witnessing that is wise witnessing is skillful and sensitive. It is alert to those decisive and crucial moments when people are open and ready to hear the Word — when they are good soil that will produce a hundredfold.

Evangelism depends not on the quantity of our efforts but the quality. It is the skill of being sensitive to that all-important right moment when the soil is good. This is what makes the difference and produces the full and abundant harvest.

### No Equal Pie

One more thing needs to be said before we leave our discussion of the soils. The temptation when first reading the parable is to picture a field divided into four equal parts. This would mean that three-fourths of the field is bad soil. There is nothing in the parable to warrant these kinds of proportions. It is not a story of sowing against impossible odds. As we first might have assumed, it is not three-to-one against the seed finding good soil.

A more accurate picture would be a field of good rich dirt. A path weaves across it. On either side of the path are thorns, and perhaps the same is true along the fence. Here and there rocks lie close to the surface. But by far the large majority of the field is good soil.

The sower, as we have pointed out above, is reckless and extravagant with his sowing, but he is no fool. The seeds which fell on the bad ground were just the spillover of a carefree and happy sower who is certain of an abundant harvest. If some seeds fall on the bad soil, at least it will provide food for the birds. The parable presents us with a sower who is generous. And so is God. God is a God of grace. The bad soil no less than the good belongs to him and he may see more potential there than we.

The important thing is not the sad fate of the relatively small amount of seed that fell on bad soil. That is God's problem and he will deal with it, in his own time, and in his own way. The important thing is the promise — the glorious announcement of what happened to the bulk of the seed that fell on the largest area of the field. It produced an abundant, an unbelievable harvest — thirty, sixty, a hundredfold. That is good news.

## The Seed

We have talked a great deal about the soils, now we look at the good seed. There were both good and bad soils, but mention is made only of good seed. The explanation of the parable identifies the good seeds as the Word of God. And it is good because ultimately it cannot be defeated either by friend or foe. The people of God may resist it, the world may oppose it, but in the end it will produce a great harvest.

To place full confidence in a little seed is not an easy thing to do. The seed is so small, and so lacking of all signs of life, that it is difficult to see the potential power packed within it. It takes faith and trust to see a future field of fertile plants locked up in a handful of shriveled seeds. The farmer learns by experience that this is so. But for us who must trust the seed of the Word, there is no experience to assure us. The harvest is yet to come. No man has seen it. Therefore, there is only seed time for us, and we must sow simply because God tells us to, and promises us that the harvest will certainly come. That takes not only faith but patience and trust.

Many times we not only lack the experience of the harvest, but we are denied ever seeing the seeds sprout forth and grow into plants. God does not promise we will always see the fruits of our labor. We are called only to sow the seed of his Word. And this, too, is not easy. Fill a football stadium with 60,000 worshipers and crowd the aisles with converts eager to confess Christ, and the power of the Word is apparent. But our task is not so glamorous. We are called to plant in the hearts of people the Word that must germinate slowly for a month or even years before it pushes its way above the ground and shows signs of life.

I remember complaining as a child about all the seeds in a watermelon. I asked my father why God couldn't have created seedless watermelons. When he explained to me how these seeds were planted and produced more watermelons, I was greatly impressed with the process, and took a few seeds and placed them by the side of my plate.

When dinner was over I couldn't wait until I could get outside and plant the seeds in my mother's rose garden. That night I got up several times and looked out of my bedroom window to see if anything was happening. In my childish enthusiasm I was sure that in the morning the whole garden would be covered with lush ripe watermelons.

So often this is the way we approach the Word of God. We want immediate results. We forget that it is only a seed. The power of it is found in its promise, "Unless a grain of wheat falls into the earth and dies, it remains alone, but if it dies it bears much fruit." (John 12:24) John here is talking of the resurrection, but it also applies to the work of the Word in general. God's work always demands patience, trust, and faith. For it is not a work of magic, but of mercy. Therefore, wait for the final fulfillment with patience, because we have confidence — full confidence — in the power of the Word. In God's own time he will bring it into new life, and in his time he will harvest it for himself.

## The Harvest

Following the rule of "end stress," many scholars like Archibald Hunter[6] find the spotlight of interpretation falling on the last item of the parable — namely the abundant harvest. In spite of frustrations, failures and opposition, God and his Kingdom will succeed and be victorious.

David Granskou[7] calls it a parable of "hope." He points out that Jesus is not the "pouting prophetic preacher" nor a "prophet of doom"; rather, he is always the young man of hopeful vision. In this parable the Lord calls his church to broader perspectives of hope.

It is true that we lose hope when we lose an overall perspective and vision. We hear a great deal about the deadening effects of television on the creative imagination. The truth is, there is a far more deadly disease — that of "tunnel vision." It is apparent in the narrow-minded, near-sighted person who cannot see beyond his own little area of self-concerns. He never takes time out and stands back to look at the whole panorama of life.

He is like the little old man from the desert. When he approached a tunnel for the first time in his life, he stopped his truck, got out, looked for several minutes into the tunnel, then got back into his truck. As he headed back the way he had come, he muttered to himself, "I could get in this end of the tunnel O.K. But I could never squeeze this truck through that little opening at the other end."

That is tunnel vision. Narrow short-sightedness. Many of us despair and lack courage, because we have no broad vision of life. Hope from the Christian point of view is not an idle wish but a confident promise. In the Parable of the Sower, Christ says that God may sow carelessly and extravagantly but he has a broad view of life. In the face of great odds and fierce opposition, he sows with his eyes on the harvest — the harvest that will surely come. This is the vision that enables us to move beyond faith to hope. The promise of the harvest will plow up the hard soil of our life, root up the rocks and the thorns and enable us to open ourselves with confidence to the falling seed. We know that the sower is loving, and the seed is good, and the harvest is certain. With so much goodness all around us, what can we do but respond and share in the promised victory of the harvest.

## Hold Fast to Faith

In the explanation which follows the text of the parable, the good soil is defined. Each Gospel writer phrases it a little differently.

Matthew says, ". . . those who hear the message and understand it." (12:13)

Luke states, ". . . those who hear the message and retain it in good and obedient hearts."

Mark puts it differently, ". . . they hear the message, accept it, and bear fruit." (Mark 4:20)

Despite the differences, all in one way or the other stress the idea of holding on to the Word once we have been given it. None of the soils initially reject the seed. They all receive it at first. So it would seem that the real point of the story is not acceptance, or rejection, but endurance. Only one soil held on to the seed and gave it a chance to grow. But how do we do this?

## The Field

The answer the parable gives to this question is found not in the sower, or the seed, or the soils alone but in the image of the field. The seeds fall together into a field where they are expected to grow together. The harvest is a product of the field. So faith as the fruit of the Word is meant to grow in relationship. Faith is never isolated and alone. It is always the product of a field of believers.

Now it is true that no one can have faith for another. But it is equally true that we cannot have faith without another. No person can hold fast to faith by himself. The Word God gives is a Word to the community — to the fellowship. He always sows his seed in a field.

The great Golden Gate Bridge of San Francisco is supported by gigantic cables. But they are not as they appear — great ribbons of steel. Rather, these cables are made up of thousands of steel wires that have been twisted together to produce this great load-bearing strength. So with us. By ourselves we cannot hold fast to faith. But bound together in a fellowship, in a fertile field, faith grows, becomes a strong, hardy plant, and produces much fruit.

Now this fellowship doesn't mean just getting together on Sunday morning and singing through the liturgy. No, it means sharing together, being mutually concerned for one another, listening to each other's problems, and helping one another in every hour of need.

Dr. Reinartz, who was for years secretary of the Lutheran Church in America, visited many churches. The people would tell him about their church. They would point out their impressive sanctuaries and Sunday school buildings. They would speak of their big budgets and generous benevolence to the work of the church. "But," says Dr. Reinartz, "the greatest thing I ever heard about a congregation came from a little old lady who said, 'Well, our building isn't much, and we struggle to meet the budget, but one thing you can say about our church is that once you join this church you never have to bear another burden alone.'"

This is the secret of holding fast to the Word. It is the field into which the seed is sown. As we are together, we are strong. So as we strive to discover the meaning of the Parable of the Sower, we should consider not only the soils, and the seed, but the intent of the Sower who sows his seeds in a field. He intends that the seeds should grow together. Some of us are not bad soil, we are just poor soil. We need help. We cannot hold fast to the Word by ourselves. God knows that we are not strong, but he gives even to the weakest a full portion of the seed. It is the field that produces the harvest, and God desires that we share in it.

Finally, then, this parable teaches us that the Word of God, together with the Kingdom of his people, will meet refusal and opposition and will experience failure, but both the Word and his Kingdom will triumph over all. God has created a field to be his Kingdom. He sows the seed of his Word into that chosen field and he knows that the harvest will come, and it will be an abundant one.

*3*

# The Waiting Game

### The Parable of the Wheat and the Tares
### Matthew 13:24-30

All of us who have tried to plant a garden or get a green lawn to grow have had the experience of putting out good plants or sowing top quality seeds, only to discover that after a short time of neglect the weeds had taken over.

Did you ever wonder where the weeds come from? Our parable says they come from the enemy. While we are asleep, in the dead of night, he comes under the cover of darkness and maliciously sows weeds in our garden.

Now to the first century Jew this would seem like a very plausible answer, for in the Orient a common means of getting revenge on a disagreeable neighbor was to sow weeds in his field. In the explanation of the parable, however (Matthew 13:36-43), the sower of the weeds is identified not as a vengeful neighbor, but as the evil one — the Devil himself.

Perhaps this causes more problems for us than the idea of where the weeds come from in the first place, for the Devil is not commonly accepted by many of us as a believable reality. We will deal with the issue of the reality of a personal Devil later. For now we want to focus in on the dramatic action of the story which centers not on the origin of the weeds (who sowed them, or where they came from), but on the issue of what we are going to do with the weeds now that they are here. How are we to react to the presence of evil in our world and in our own lives?

The simple and direct answer of the parable is that we are to wait — wait until the harvest. Then the time of separation will come.

## The Waiting Game

The waiting game is certainly not the most popular sport. In fact, to wait for someone is perhaps one of the most exasperating things we have to do.

In this age of constant rushing, where we hurry through a workweek for the relief of the weekend, or through a workday for the welcomed coffee break and the whistle that brings our workday to an end, we all become clock watchers. Waiting for the traffic light to change when we are late can irritate the most even-tempered. Waiting in a long line at the supermarket can ruin our whole day. Yet playing the "waiting game," our parable tells us, is a very vital part of being a member of the Kingdom of God.

Christians have long been told to "wait for the Lord," to hold back, endure, have patience and look to the future. But this biding our time and passively resigning ourselves to what is happening, particularly when what is happening is wrong, is never easy. Any soldier will tell you that the most difficult times in any battle are the hours of waiting for the battle to begin.

The Israelites played the "waiting game." They waited, not always with patience, for over fifty years of enduring exile, homelessness, and near starvation. They plodded through one ordinary day after another in the wilderness. They waited for deliverance. They waited for the promised land. They waited for the Messiah. Yet, as one prominent Hebrew scholar has pointed out, it was undoubtedly this waiting on the Lord that built into the very fiber of the Jewish nation the faith to face the disappointments and persecutions which have been their continual lot in history.

The important thing for any people is to discover the positive aspect of waiting — to see that waiting is not just holding back, biding time, or doing nothing, but can be a positive action. Waiting is positive when it is accompanied by a promise. Waiting is positive when you know that there is something ahead worth waiting for.

Every year Charlie Brown of the "Peanuts" comic strip finds himself tempted to kick the football that Lucy holds for him. Charlie's response after many times being foiled by Lucy is to turn his face to heaven and cry out, "How long? Oh Lord!" But with the hope that things will be different this season, he makes a mad dash toward the ball. His hope is shattered as Lucy jerks the ball away and Charlie thumps the ground, once again the fool. Lucy chides him, "How long? All your life, Charlie Brown, all your life."

This "waiting game" that God calls his people to play is not like that faced by Charlie Brown. Oh, we may, like Charlie, be foiled again and again. Like Charlie, our waiting may have its lumps and its bruises, but God is no Lucy who chides us. Rather, he comforts and encourages us. And more, he promises us that waiting is not all there is to life in His Kingdom. Waiting is just the beginning. As our Lord said to his disciples, ". . . for a little while." The Kingdom is coming and it is worth waiting for.

To wait is not easy, but when we have something worth waiting for, then it can be done with patience. Waiting can be a positive action when we catch the vision of what great things are in store for us. With such a vision we can, like little children, anxiously wait for the party or the picnic with excitement and joy. We know that what our Father promises he will fulfill.

With this attitude let us turn to a discussion of the Parable of the Wheat and the Tares and listen and learn its lesson.

## The Field

We begin our discussion where the parable begins — in the field. Jesus, when he explains the parable to his disciples (Matthew 13:36-43), identifies the field as the world. Later, however, he equates it with the Kingdom (verse 41) when he says, "The Son of Man will send his angels and they will gather up out of his Kingdom all who cause people to sin . . ."

C. H. Dodd[1] interprets the field as the "church." Jeremias[2] sees the field as the "disciples" and views the parable as an answer Christ gives to his critics as they find fault with the caliber and quality of men chosen as disciples. Gerald Kennedy[3] points out that the field represents those of us who have within ourselves both wheat and tares.

Emil Brunner[4] recognizes the main theme of the parable to be the Kingdom of God. And, he adds, the Kingdom exists not only in the world at large, but also in the church and within each individual. Wherever God rules and wherever his will is done, there is the Kingdom. For Brunner the field of the parable is not so much analogous to a place as it is to history — the history of the entire world, the church, and the individual. The field is pictured in the parable as a battle between the reign of God and the reign of evil.

The important issue of the parable thereby becomes not the distinction between a world of weeds and the church where only wheat grows. The issue is the conflict between God and the Evil One which rages in every area of life, in the church as well as in the world.

## The Devil

One of the assumptions of the parable is that our Lord was a man of his times and believed in the Devil as a personal reality. He was not struggling against fate, or impersonal forces, or wrong ideas, or bad social conditions; he was fighting a personal will that was in deliberate rebellion against

God.

The power possessed by evil was over man, but under the authority of God. This was not a dualism of equally matched forces battling for supremacy. This was a revolution within God's Kingdom. Christ therefore saw his task as twofold: to free imprisoned humankind from the Devil, then meet the Evil One face to face and attack and defeat him for all time so that there could once more be peace and harmony within God's Kingdom.

Now the concept of a personal Devil is difficult for most of us to understand. When the average person mentions the Devil, it is generally in jest, such as Flip Wilson saying, "The Devil made me do it." Part of our difficulty is that we have associated the Evil One with the picture of a fellow in a red flannel suit with horns, pitch fork and a long pointed tail. This is a product not of the Scriptures but of medieval imagination expressed in folklore and legend.

In the New Testament in general and in our parable in particular, just the opposite is true. The Evil One is not obvious and easily recognized. He is subtle and cunning and looks just about like everyone else.

One of the decisive points of the parable is that the wheat and tares look so much alike, especially in the early stage. By the time the plants come to a head and it is easy to distinguish them, it is too late. The roots of the wheat and the tares are so intertwined that pulling up the tares will tear the wheat out with them. So the Devil is deceptive. He is extremely clever. This, then, is one of the essential characteristics of evil that suggests a person rather than a static force or predictable power which works from a principle of cause and effect.

When the men of the New Testament present evil as a person, this is their way of expressing the flexibility and maneuverability of evil. It can react, adjust, and adapt to any and all situations that might arise. To enter the ring and challenge evil is not to box with shadows, but to face a skillful opponent who can duck and dodge and hit back when your guard is down.

The men of the New Testament were keenly aware of the cunningness and trickery they had experienced in their encounters with evil. And there was no better way to express this quality of evil than to personify it. The Bible advises us to deal with evil as if we were dealing with a person.

German theologians, when considering what happened in Germany under the reign of Hitler, have pointed out that the end result cannot be explained by simply adding up all the persons involved and combing their potential evil. There was something super-social about their experience with evil.

After the war I visited a concentration camp. The pastor who was showing me around took me into a concrete-block building. It was one large room with faucet-like fixtures jutting out from the walls. He shoved a bench over to the side walls and motioned me to stand on it. When I did, he said, "Notice the strange marking on the wall about ten feet from the floor." I looked and saw there were curious indentations into the concrete, like some unidentifiable lettering. "Can you read that?" he asked. "No, I imagine not." Then to my horror he explained, "This building was a gas chamber during the war. Each day hundreds of Jews were led naked into this room thinking that it was a shower. When the doors were closed and bolted, deadly gas hissed through those jets. When the people realized what was happening they panicked. Those markings cut deep into solid concrete were the marks of human fingernails made by those terrified people as they frantically tried to claw their way out."

Now such examples of man's inhumanity to man are ample evidence that the power of evil cannot be explained or accounted for, by adding up the sum total of potential evil of the German people. Evil is super-social. That is one of the things that the Bible is witnessing to when it personifies evil and presents the image of a personal Devil.

The flexibility, the adaptability, the cleverness, the cunningness of evil are vital and helpful insights concerning the nature of evil in our world. And we are foolish to close our ears to this profound insight into a people's experience of evil simply because we are turned off by the image of a personal Devil.

## The Devil's Little Acre

There is also within the parable an assumption that the Devil chooses to work where God is most active. He does not fence off a section of the world for his own little acre. Rather, he deliberately plants his tares in the very field that God is cultivating.

There is a tendency for religious people in general and church people in particular to talk as if evil selects a certain prescribed territory in which to set up his business. We refer to these places as a "den of iniquity," or a "dive," or a "brothel." To enter such places is to open ourselves up to temptation. The parable indicates, however, that there is no zone of security from the work of evil. The Devil works in the church as well as in the dimly lit dives down dark alleys. In fact, the Evil One prefers Holy Places — God's field — for there he can fully utilize his artful disguises and exercise his full bag of tricks. The faithful believer is not immune from the Devil; rather is he the Devil's prize objective.

They tell the story about saintly old Dr. Greaver, who was for years an outstanding leader of the church. One morning at 7 o'clock he called up a young minister, "Are you up yet, Kenneth?" Dr. Greaver inquired. "Well, you better be, 'cause the Devil is."

So the church is the Devil's parish as well as God's, and we labor not only **for** God but **against** the Devil. The parable says, don't be surprised to find tares among the wheat — expect them there. For weeds like and thrive on the same fertile ground as do the good plants. Both wheat and weed grow together.

## What to Do About It

According to most scholars the Parable of the Wheat and

the Tares is not intended primarily to prove either the existence of a personal Devil, or the presence of evil in our world, our church, or within ourselves. It is rather directed to the problem of what, if anything, we should do with the evil that is among us.

## Patience

Jeremias[5] expresses the opinion of the majority of scholars concerning the major thrust of the parable with his little phrase, "the exhortation to patience." Or as we have said at the beginning of our discussion, the answer is that we are "to wait."

Granskou[6] says we are not to "over-react." Kennedy[7] puts it, "We must learn to live with imperfections." Many suggestive ideas come when we study the various approaches people have given to the question "Why" and "How" we are to wait.

## Why Wait?

The answer the parable gives is that we are to wait because, "As you gather the weeds you might pull up some of the wheat along with them." Interpreters start with this answer and then proceed to expand upon it, thereby creating many rich insights into the parable as a story.

### The Whole Goose

Luther calls for an overall view of the Kingdom. Our reaction to any particular problem should be seen in the light of this big view of faith. He stresses that many times we must be willing to suffer in a cause that will ultimately win, rather than to enjoy immediate success in a cause that will ultimately fail. We should not be disturbed by small concerns and anxieties in our private lives, but having caught the wide vision of God's sovereignty, rejoice in patience.

Luther pointed out that we should always consider what our actions will do to the whole body of citizens. We should punish evil within the bounds of good judgment and never thoughtlessly rush head-on into rash actions that might only result in our destroying each other. "The householder," says Luther, "will never grow rich who because one has plucked a feather from his goose, flings the whole goose after him."[8]

## God Uses Evil

Zwingli[9] takes a rather unusual approach to the issue of evil in this parable. He believes that we should wait and not root out evil because God may use evil to our own advantage. God sometimes uses evil to mature and increase our faith. This does not mean that God desires to use evil for his work, or that God creates evil for his own advantage. But once evil does exist and is operative in creation because of man's rebellion, God can and does use it for good.

The cross, for example, was constructed by man to punish evildoers. But God takes this instrument of punishment and fashions out of it a means of redemption.

Rusken was spending the weekend at the home of a lady who had a very rare and valuable collection of handkerchiefs. One of the guests had brought a magnificent handkerchief to give her hostess as a thank-you gift. While she was writing the accompanying note, a large drop of ink fell from the pen into the very center of the handkerchief. The artist Ruskin, seeing her tearful disappointment, asked to borrow the handkerchief. He took his paints, and starting with the ink blot as the basic pattern, he fashioned of it a magnificent design in the center of the fabric. Today that ink-blotted handkerchief resides in a museum, the choice piece of a very distinguished collection. So God takes the ink blots of our lives and uses them as the basis for a creation of beauty.

## Judgment

Hunter[10] believes that we are to wait because weeding implies judgment and judgment is the exclusive right of God and God alone. We are not qualified to separate the good from the bad. We cannot look into the heart of a person. We see only the outward manifestations of wickedness, but we cannot tell what is really happening. It may be that a decisive struggle is going on within a person. We see only the surface turmoil and fail to see that God is at work within the person bringing him to redemption. We condemn what God is redeeming.

## No Harm Done

Wallace[11] says that we are to wait, for there is no quick and easy solution to the problem of evil. He agrees with Hunter that dealing with evil is too great a task for us. It is God-size in its proportions.

Like the little boy in the yard with his father, pulling up weeds — the little boy wanted to impress his father and took hold of the weed and pulled with all his strength but it wouldn't budge. Seeing the little boy's distress, his father walked over to him and said, "Weed pulling is a tough job, son, because the whole world has hold of the other end."

So the task of pulling up evil is no easy job. In fact, it is too great a task for us. But then Wallace adds a positive note. Even though the tares obscure the wheat, they cannot damage the good crop. There is no indication in the parable that the wheat suffers because of the weeds. The weeds do not rob moisture or nutrition from the wheat. Therefore, let the weeds grow, for they do no harm to anything but themselves. For as the weeds grow, it becomes more and more apparent what they are.

God sets decisive limits on evil. He permits it a certain degree of success, for only in this way will evil really reveal itself for what it is. When God thinks evil is ripe, he will destroy it. Therefore, trust God, for the Kingdom of God exists not where there is only righteousness and obedience. Rather, the Kingdom exists where people trust God and know that evil will ultimately fail.

## No Delay

Dodd,[12] looking at the parable from the point of view of realized eschatology, gives the optimistic note that the harvest (the final coming of the Kingdom) is not delayed because there are weeds in the field.

The coming of the Kingdom is itself the process of sifting out the weeds. Any idea on our part that destroying the weeds will bring the Kingdom closer is presumptuous. It is an insult to the Christ who humbled himself and came to this world to bring in the Kingdom of God.

Some people take up arms and declare war on evil as if by doing so they are deciding the destiny of the Kingdom. They cry out for moral rearmament. They are like angry little old ladies in tennis shoes, marching into bars, smashing bottles of booze with righteous indignation — as if the problem of evil could ever be solved by breaking bottles or making anything less available to the sensuous desires of human beings.

The problem of evil is not the "things" of this world, but the satanic ability of evil persons to pervert and misuse all the good things of God's creation. The problem of evil is not what people do, but what they **are**. We can no more rid the world of evil by our own efforts than we can change people. Moral reform may clean up our society and make life more comfortable and pleasant; therefore, it is a worthwhile work. But when we delude ourselves into thinking that this is the solution to the problem of evil in our world, we are headed for a faith-shattering disillusionment.

If you want a good example of this, just try mowing the tops off of the weeds with your lawnmower and see if that rids your lawn of weeds. It might look good for a while but the weeds will grow back healthier than before. You must get to the roots of the weeds and destroy them. And only God can do that.

So evil as a force and power in our world cannot be destroyed by our efforts no matter how much immediate success our reforms may enjoy. Only a cross on a lonely hill, and an empty tomb in a garden, and the coming of Jesus in glory can accomplish the gigantic job of rooting out and destroying evil.

## Correcting Wrongs

At this point Calvin[13] is helpful as he points out that this parable does not prohibit us from correcting wrongs in our world and working against evil forces. He quotes Cyprian, "Let man then mercifully correct what he can: what he cannot correct let him bear patiently."

Calvin agrees that God alone can eliminate evil, but we nevertheless have a duty to combat the effects of evil in our world. When we do this we are not destroying evil so much as we are witnessing to the ultimate work of God who will, when the time is right, rid the field of the weeds and gather the wheat unto himself.

Perhaps the key to understanding what we cannot do when we come up against evil in our world is the phrase, "Pull up the weeds," which literally means destroy, eliminate, kill. This we cannot do. But we can combat evil and take our stand against it.

When Sherman marched to the sea, a little old lady refused to leave her home in Georgia. She stood on her front porch and watched the fields and the homes of her neighbors burning across the valley. As the army of Sherman came closer and closer and finally started down the road to her farm, she could restrain herself no longer. She grabbed her broom and stood defiantly in the road. The advancing soldiers stopped and the captain cried out to her, "Old lady, do you expect to win the war with a broom?" "No," came the quick reply, "but at least I'll show the world which side I'm on."

So we combat the effects of evil in our world not because we are deluded into thinking that we can ever rid the world of evil. We know that we can't. Only God can do that. But as we stand up against evil with our little brooms, we show the world which side we're on. We stand with God who possesses the power to overcome the Evil One, and to put down all those who rise up in rebellion against him.

### How Are We to Wait?

This leads us to how we are to wait. We have pointed out that this parable does not imply non-resistance to the effects of evil in our world. We are to wait, but we are to actively wait. It remains now to define the shape of our resistance and the manner of our waiting. Brunner helps us here. When he interprets this parable he comes to the conclusion that we are to resist evil not by forceful action, judgment, or uprooting, but by the strength of faith, prayer, obedience and loyalty to God. Brunner says, "The only way to really do battle against evil within this world is to constantly remember that we belong to God."[14]

We are to resist evil not with **force** but with **faith**. We oppose evil by our trust in Christ. Evil does not fear us or our efforts. Evil fears only Christ. So we are to wait positively and patiently. We are to actively wait in true faith, clinging to the promise and the cross of Christ. Fear not the hold evil has on our world. Remember only that one greater than evil has hold of us and he will never let us go.

### God Is Sovereign

This parable speaks to the temptation in all of us to take matters into our own hands. It warns us that God is sovereign, and we should avoid taking over God's business.

When the parable is viewed simply as story some interesting points emerge. We see that it is the man who owns the field that sowed the seeds. Why not the servants? Was not that task their responsibility? In all the normal everyday situation of farming it would have been the servants who sowed the seeds and not the owner. Then the servants come and ask if they should pull up the weeds. The people who first heard this story would have been surprised. Any farm worker worth his salt would have known that you never pull darnel up when it is growing among the wheat. The farm owner states very emphatically, "I will tell the harvest workers." Note that he does not say to the servants, "I will tell you to pull up the weeds when the time comes." And the story ends with the note, "in **my** barns."

Each step of the story clearly places the full weight of the plot on the owner of the field. At best the servants play a supportive role. Even the enemy is not identified in the story itself. It is as if everything is designed by the storyteller to place exclusive attention on the owner of the field. He sows, he instructs the servants, he tells the harvest workers, he gathers into his barns.

As a story the parable has but one conclusion. It says to the listener, "Hands off, don't interfere. The weeds are the owner's business."

A secondary implication of the story is that the servants will do more harm to the wheat than the enemy if they persist and interfere, trying to correct the situation. The enemy only sowed weeds among wheat which causes extra work and effort at harvest time, but it does not harm the wheat. On the other hand, if the servants try to undo what the enemy has done, they will actually harm and destroy the wheat. The implication here is that well-meaning servants can do more harm by trying to help than the enemy did in the first place by sowing the weeds.

The first lesson drawn from such an implication would be a warning to us that when we attempt to interfere in the activities that exclusively belong to God we are God's worst enemies. There is a familiar saying, "Save me from my friends, I can take care of my enemies," or another equally as familiar, "with friends like this who needs enemies?"

A man was struggling with a large box on the back edge of

his truck. A passing neighbor saw his plight and came over to help him. He put his shoulder to the box. After a few tiring moments the neighbor exclaimed, "What's in that box anyway? I don't think we'll ever get it on the truck." "Get it on!" the exasperated man shouted, "I'm trying to get it off!"

So the parable speaks to those who would serve God. Don't take matters into your own hands. Don't serve without directives and orders, or you will in most cases be working against God rather than for him.

Well-meaning Christians can be God's worst enemies. When we judge and condemn others, when we set up our own standards of what it means to be saved, when we claim absolute knowedge of God's will and of his Scriptures, we take over God's role and attempt to run his business. This parable makes it quite clear who is boss. God is. And he will tolerate no interference with his absolute authority. Therefore, we should never forget we are servants and strive only to serve him by getting out of the way so that he can accomplish his work.

The second lesson this parable teaches concerns salvation. Our salvation and the salvation of the world is the work of God and God alone. Both we and our world will be saved by grace and by grace alone. When we attempt to interfere and do something to save ourselves, we only frustrate the work of grace in us.

As when a person is drowning and the lifeguard comes to his aid, any effort on the part of the drowning man to save himself only works against the efforts of the one who is in the process of attempting to save him.

The parable states in bold, broad statements that God is sovereign in all things. He and he alone is the one who shall rid the world of evil. And he and he alone shall save us — gather us into his barns at the harvest time.

Salvation is by grace and by grace alone. We are not saved by **our** strong faith, or **our** obedient servanthood. We are saved only when we stand back and let God do it.

# 4

# Striking It Rich

### The Parables of the Treasure and the Pearl
### Matthew 13:44-52

These two parables should touch a responsive note in most of us because they are stories about two men who struck it rich. Isn't this the dream of us all, to be the lucky person who wins the lottery, the magazine sweepstakes, or bets on the winning horse? What happened to these two men could happen to us, because after all, it was just a matter of dumb luck. It happened in the ordinary routine of going about their daily chores. The farmer was plowing in his field, and the merchant was working at his trade of buying and selling precious gems. Then it happened. Suddenly their lives were changed by the chance finding of a fortune.

Jesus introduces these two parables with the familiar phrase, "The Kingdom of God is like . . ." And then he goes on to say that the Kingdom is like **finding** a treasure in a field and a precious pearl. The stories are not about two men seeking a fortune but accidentally **finding** a treasure.

When Jesus first told these parables, they must have pleased the crowds but disturbed the religious leaders, for they make fools out of every scribe and Pharisee who spent most of their lives searching the Scriptures for clues of how to find the Kingdom, and how to identify it once it was found. In the two stories the men were just going about their daily business, and the treasure came to them like a stroke of sheer dumb luck. And says Jesus, "This is what the Kingdom of God is like."

And this is a very different message from what we're used to hearing. Faith is so often presented as seeking after goodness and the best in life. If we are to find the Kingdom, we need to prepare ourselves, to turn our backs on bad company, give up evil habits and improve our image. We need to show God we are serious about this business of religion and therefore worthy of his attention. We are advised to roll up our sleeves and move away from normalcy to a more spiritually oriented style of life. But here is Christ saying that the Kingdom of God comes not to those who are best prepared but to two fellows doing their daily jobs and not even thinking about the treasure that is about to surprise them.

Many scholars like Hunter[1] draw a distinction between the farmer and the merchant, that whereas the farmer stumbled over the treasure in his field, the merchant was really out searching for the great pearl. Now undoubtedly the merchant always dreamed of finding a prize pearl but we really can't say that he was searching for it. The day he discovered the pearl he was simply engaged in buying and selling run-of-the-mill gems. Then suddenly he saw a pearl that took his breath away. He was just as surprised as the farmer.

There are some differences between the farmer and the merchant. One man was a rich merchant and the other a poor dirt farmer. Some interpreters have seen in this the two extremes of society and conclude that the lesson here expressed is that the Kingdom of God is for all people, rich and poor.

Then there is a difference in the situation when the treasure and the pearl are found. Everyone who knew anything about gems knew that the great pearl was a prized possession. The merchant was willing to buy it against competition. It was a deal transacted entirely in the open arena of business. But there is a shady side to the farmer's discovery. The parable points out that he quickly covered the treasure up so that no one would know that he had found it. Then he went and bought the field at a bargain price assuming that the owner had no idea of what the field contained.

Now we might conclude from this that the Kingdom of God comes to crooked characters as well as to honest businessmen. However, some who point out this difference find in the farmer's action an example of buying something that no one else wants. Because he knows its inner value, he is willing to be called a fool for sacrificing everything for a field that is apparently worthless. They then conclude that Jesus directed this parable to the disciples. He was saying, in effect, don't be discouraged when people laugh at you for giving up everything and following me. You have chosen the better way. The people think that they are rich and you have nothing. The truth is you have everything and it is they who are poor. Your treasure is hidden for the moment within you. Therein is the Kingdom of God begun. It is a secret treasure now, but one day it will be revealed and all people will know the wisdom of your choice and the foolishness of theirs.

These differences are interesting to note, but they are overshadowed by the striking similarity of the two parables. Both are stories about men who were bold and decisive. They saw what they wanted and were willing to do anything to get it.

### The Pearl of Great Value

The parable begins: the Kingdom of God is like finding a pearl of great price and a treasure of great cost. Because of this it is commonly called the Parable of the Pearl of Great Price. But it might be better entitled the Pearl of Great Value. There is a difference between price and value and the difference is vital in discovering the full thrust of these parables.

Oscar Wilde once said, "Americans know the price of everything and the value of nothing." Price is the cost you have to pay to get something you want. Value is what something is really worth. And these are not always the same. Let us look first at price.

## The Price Is High

The parable points out that the price of both the pearl and the treasure was mighty high. Both men, the farmer and the merchant, had to go out and sell everything they had in order to own what they had found. Many interpreters have seen in this the lesson of sacrifice. The Kingdom of God, they conclude, demands of us a great sacrifice. Eta Linnemann,[2] however, does not agree. She points out that there is a difference between a sacrifice and a purchase price. A sacrifice, in the Christian sense, is giving that expects no reward or profit. In our stories the merchant and the farmer were buying something that they knew was worth more than what they were paying for it. Therefore, what they did was pay a purchase price — not make a sacrifice.

Whatever word you use to describe their actions, the point of the story in each case was that they had to sell everything in order to get what they had found. And whether you know you are going to make a profit or not, the giving up of everything you have demands bold and decisive action.

## The Price Is Right

The price is high, but the price is right because, given the courage, we can afford it. It doesn't demand more than we have, only all we have. In this day of credit cards that enable us to live beyond our means, we often spend more than we have. When we want something of great cost, we don't sell everything we have — we go in debt. In the parable, however, there is no extended credit or the borrowing of money in order to acquire the pearl or the treasure. The men have the price in the possessions that already belong to them.

So with us. What the Kingdom demands, we have. For it is ourselves. God gives us our life and now he asks that we give it back to him in order to possess the Kingdom of God within us.

The price is also right because it involves a joyful giving. When some people hear that the Kingdom of God demands that we give all we have in order to possess it, they view this as a painful oblation of self-denial, the putting on of sackcloth and ashes. For the men in the parables there is no mood of martyrdom about what they have to do. Rather there is a mood of excitement and joy. The merchant and the farmer do not say, "Wouldn't you know it. For the first time in my life fortune smiles on me, and I find something worth having, and I have to go out and sell all I have to get it." No! The implication of the parables is that each man was so excited that he could hardly wait to sell everything in order to get the treasure he had found. The "giving up all" is a happy action. Eta Linnemann phrases it, "These men realize they are facing a unique opportunity."[3] The dominant mood of the parable is that selling all to buy the discovered prize is an act of celebration. Just as God rejoices when the lost lamb is found, so a person celebrates when the Kingdom is discovered. He carries out the task of making the Kingdom his own like the shepherd carries the lamb on his shoulders — a joyous work!

## The Value of the Pearl

This leads us from the cost to the value of the pearl and the treasure, and therein lies one of the central points of the parable.

An old man went into an antique shop and it was quite apparent from the way he was dressed that he had entered an exclusive and expensive shop selling objects of art well beyond his means. He looked about the shop carefully. The next day he came back and looked again. Finally, he selected an oriental vase and asked the shopkeeper if he could put it on lay-away and pay for it a few dollars each week. The owner was fascinated by the little old man so he agreed. Week after week for about three years the man came into the shop and made his payments. Finally, the vase was paid for. As the little old man was leaving the shop, the owner could resist his curiosity no longer, so he asked, "Please do not think me rude, but it is rather obvious that you really can't afford this expensive vase. Why then are you so determined to buy it?" Without hesitation, the little old man answered, "Well, as you can see, I am very poor. I live on a small pension in a tiny little room down the street. And when I first moved into that room, knowing that I would spend the rest of my life there, I decided I would put in it only that which was the very best."

So in our parables once the men had seen the prize, discovered the pearl, uncovered the treasure, they knew it was the very best. And they had to have it. No one had to sell it to them. They knew immediately that they must have it. No one had to argue with them, or convince them, or beg them to strive for the treasure and the pearl. No! To see it was a compulsion to have it. The power was in the pearl and the chest of treasure.

Barclay[4] points out that at the time of Jesus pearls were the most valuable of all gems. They were what diamonds are today, a most sought-after possession. For here is a form of wealth that possesses its own inherent beauty and attractiveness. For example, it is said of the Hope Diamond that you do not have to sell it. You just have to find someone who can afford it. You don't have to convince anyone that the Hope Diamond is valuable, or beautiful, or a desirable possession. All you have to do is show it. The Hope Diamond sells itself.

So with the pearl and the treasure of the Kingdom, the power is within it to create within a person the desire to possess it. When the Kingdom of God is seen — really seen — it is irresistible. When Hillary was asked why he climbed Mt.

Everest, he answered, "Because it was there." And that is why the merchant and the farmer sold everything to purchase their discovery. The sight of what they found was irresistible. The parables are stories about the power of the Kingdom of God over humankind. The important thing is not what we have to do to get it, but what it does to us once we have seen it. The power of the Kingdom is irresistible. It makes all our present possessions appear as poverty.

## Never See It

If the Kingdom of God is irresistible, why then do so many not sell all they have to make it their own? According to the parable it is not due to their unwillingness to pay the price. For this is not a doublet story about two men, one who found a great pearl and was willing to pay the price for it, and the other about a man who found a hidden treasure and was not willing to pay the price. Rather, it is the account of two men, one rich and the other poor, who each responded in the same way. They had to have what they found regardless of cost. Why? Because the power that motivated them did not originate in themselves but in what they had found.

So the only answer as to why people refuse to give up all for the Kingdom is, according to the parable, that they have never really seen it. They may have seen poor, distorted images of the Kingdom. They may have been presented with dime store copies of the great pearl. They may have been conned into buying fake treasure maps. But they have never seen the real thing.

You don't have to work with unchurched people very long to realize their appalling lack of a true vision of the Kingdom of God. In some cases, their first view of God was that of a celestial policeman who parents said would punish them if they did wrong. Or they have experienced God used as a means of revenge, as when Maude shouts at Walter, "God will get you for that."

Many equate going to church as experiencing the Kingdom. And church is where they were forced to go as children, where they had to sit still on a hard pew, be quiet and listen to something they couldn't understand.

Others have been brought up on the theology, "If you're having fun you must be doing something wrong." Most have been raised on a diet of "prepared-the-night-before" Sunday school lessons and have been bored by sermons that were read, poorly read, and not worth reading. Is it any wonder with such a view of the Kingdom of God, they are unwilling to sell all and make it their own?

The greatest task, when confronted with the challenge to witness for Christ and his Kingdom, is all the clearing out of rubbish and overgrowth of false concepts and mistaken ideas that have accumulated.

The job of witnessing is not to badger, argue, or beg people into making the Kingdom their own. Rather, our real task is simply to present the Kingdom so that people might see it for what it really is. Christ says, "If I be lifted up I will draw all men unto me." So with the Kingdom of God. Truly and accurately shown forth it draws and attracts people willingly and joyfully to give up everything in order to possess it. The Parables of the Pearl and the Treasure point out that people are most effectively brought into the Kingdom not by incrimination but by **fascination**.

When the hidden treasure of the Kingdom is uncovered and the precious pearl is revealed, people will respond like steel flying to a magnet, or like a hungry man's movement toward food.

And remember, the Kingdom of God will be revealed in the most unusual and yet the most ordinary of circumstances. As it came to a merchant in the market place, and to a man plowing a field, so it came to a woman at the well, and to an old saint while fishing, and to a Zacchaeus perched in a tree, and to a Paul falling from his horse, and to a Luther when the lightning flashes and frightens him. So God comes today in the strange and the ordinary. He comes to reveal his Kingdom and release its power. Therefore, be open to surprises. God's grace will not stay buried in a field, nor lie hidden in the market place. The Holy Spirit has come to uncover and make known that which has been hidden. God is loose in the world, and he desires that all people "strike it rich."

## Summary

In both stories there are three decisive turning points upon which the plot depends: finding, selling and buying. Finding is the way the Kingdom comes to us. It is an encounter which just happens. We do not pray for it, or work for it, or even search for it. We stumble across it in the daily activities of ordinary living. But when it happens, it changes us. We sell all that we have. Which means we give up all that we once were and are. Finding the Kingdom becomes a turning point in our lives. We are converted. Our whole life takes on a new direction. Then we "buy in," which means this new thing that has found us must now become ours. As we are emptied of self in the selling, we are filled with a new self in the buying. The Kingdom becomes ours by making us a part of it.

These three actions are what the Kingdom of God is like, finding, selling, and buying. They are not what we do but what happens to us as God's grace works in us. God encounters us, empties us, and then fills us with new life. These two parables are illustrations of the triumph of God's free grace. When we finally experience finding the Kingdom, selling all, and buying it for our own, we know that it is not "dumb luck" that has enabled us to "strike it rich." Rather, it has been the result of a living God who enabled us by his grace to find him and his Kingdom. The selling of all we have and are, and the buying into the Kingdom are not something we do, but something God's grace accomplishes within us.

Finally, when we look at these two parables through the Cross, we can fully know what it really means to "strike it rich." For then we can fully understand that the Kingdom we have found, sold everything to buy, is really the Kingdom of Christ who, on the cross, found us, gave his precious body and blood to purchase us, and now possesses us for his own.

# 5

# Fantastic Forgiveness

### The Parable of the Unforgiving Servant
### Matthew 18:21-35

Most of us live ordinary lives, for we never have the opportunity to do anything else. Our parable is the story of a man who had his big opportunity for greatness and he muffed it. The key to understanding the parable is the character of the man himself. He was by nature an unforgiving man, and even when he had an extraordinary experience of forgiveness, he was not changed by it. He was the same person he was before he experienced fantastic forgiveness.

### The Stage Is Set

Most of us picture Christ as a rather easy-going, mild-mannered person, never getting too excited, always maintaining his composure. For the most part this is true, but there were exceptions, and because they are exceptions, they demand from us special attention. The setting of our parable is a good example of such an occasion when Jesus lost his cool.

Matthew tells us the disciples were having a first century

buzz session. Their topic was forgiveness, and they were trying to determine how many times a man could forgive his fellow man and still fulfill the will of God. They could arrive at no agreement, so one of them suggested that Peter put the question to Christ. Peter didn't have to be encouraged. He was always ready to push an issue or put a question. So he walked up to Christ and blurted out, "Lord, how often shall my brother sin against me and I forgive him? As many as seven times?"

The explosive reaction that resulted surprised them all. For what to them was a very casual speculation was to Christ a matter of excited, almost angry concern. Peter had said, ". . . as many as seven times," indicating that he thought that he was being most generous. Christ's eyes glistened as he retorted, "I do not say to you seven times, but seventy times seven." Now this expression, ". . . seventy times seven . . .," was a current phrase used in the time of our Lord to indicate in the most emphatic possible way the idea that the action under consideration was unlimited — totally and completely unlimited.

This was Jesus' way of telling the disciples that this was nothing to speculate about. Their very concern to calculate and count the number of times we are to forgive was absolutely wrong, because it missed the whole idea of what forgiveness really meant. Any limitations placed on forgiveness destroy true forgiveness.

I remember as a child an experience with my cousin. One day I went out into the yard with a peanut butter and jelly sandwich. When my cousin saw it, he wanted a bite. I was willing to be generous — but not too generous. So I placed my thumb on the sandwich indicating just how much my cousin could have. Ignoring my limited generosity, he opened his mouth and bit down right in the middle of my thumb. So the apostle Peter got bit. Christ came down hard on Peter's attempt to limit forgiveness.

## Forgiveness not an Exception

It was obvious to Christ that the disciples did not understand forgiveness. They were taking the position that forgiveness was the exception, because the natural thing for a person to be was unforgiving. What they were actually asking was how many times they should make an exception and forgive a person. On the other hand, Christ understood forgiveness as the natural reaction of a forgiving person. The forgiven person becomes a **forgiving** person, not just a nice guy who forgives an unusually large number of times. The very fact that the disciples were asking the question showed that they were missing the real meaning of forgiveness.

The multi-millionaire, J. P. Morgan, was once asked by a friend how much it cost to maintain his yacht. Morgan snapped back, "If you have to ask the cost you can't afford it." This was the situation with the disciples. The very fact that they were speculating and calculating how many times they had to forgive indicated they were missing the whole meaning of forgiveness.

We do not know if the disciples learned their lesson or not, but Christ wanted to make sure, so he followed his remarks with a very pointed parable. It should be noted that Luke records the exchange between Christ and his disciples on the matter of forgiveness, but Matthew alone records the parable. It is considered by many scholars to be Matthew's "great parable."

Traditionally, it is called the Parable of the Unforgiving Servant. Jeremias[1] entitles it "The Unfaithful Servant." Linnemann[2] calls it "The Unmerciful Servant." But whatever title you give it, it is a good story, and we are grateful to Matthew for giving it to us. Let us look at it as a drama in three acts.

## Act One

The first act begins with a day of reckoning, and a king

who desires to settle accounts with his servants. Because of this, Jeremias[3] refers to this as a parable about the Last Judgment. For him, God has freely given us in the Gospels his offer of forgiveness. But Jeremias adds that the parable treats forgiveness as a gift with a warning. For God will revoke his forgiveness, if we do not wholeheartedly share that forgiveness with our brother who is in debt to us.

It should be noted that at the beginning of the parable the main character is the king. The temptation is to identify the king with God. In most rabbinic parables the image of a king is the symbol for God, but in this parable many problems are created by such an identification. For if the king is God, then even though Christ is pointing out to his disciples in the strongest possible way that forgiveness was **not** to be limited, but the spontaneous expression of a loving and forgiving heart, then God did not exhibit unlimited forgiveness. In the story, the forgiveness of the king is conditional and limited. In the story, the king forgives the servant his extravagant debt, but he does **not** forgive the servant his lack of forgiveness. This would be saying that God forgives us when we offend him, but when we turn around and offend him by failing to forgive others, God cannot forgive this. Therefore, God's forgiveness is limited to those who forgive others.

Such a view of God's forgiveness would be the same calculating and legalistic approach to forgiveness which Jesus so flatly and directly condemns in his disciples. The disciples were at fault when they asked, "How many times?" because such a question limited forgiveness. Certainly Christ would not then tell a story about how God's forgiveness is limited only to those who deserve or merit forgiveness by their virtuous acts of forgiving others. If the disciples are to forgive spontaneously from a heart of love, how much more will God's forgiveness be unlimited, for it spontaneously overflows from a heart that is pure love.

The gospel declares mercy to those who do not deserve it, love to the unlovely, and forgiveness to those without merit or goodness. "While we were yet sinners, Christ dies for us."

The point of the parable cannot be this legalistic juggling of the books, trying to make debts and payments of forgiveness come into balance. What the parable is saying is far more profound than a simple warning against a deed unforgiven, as we shall see later on in our discussion.

As the parable unfolds, the term "king" is dropped by Matthew and the word "lord" is used, and the story becomes an exchange between a master and his servants which is more typical of the language used by Jesus.

The important thing to remember in this parable is that the king is not to be identified with God. It is rather intended to illustrate an experience within the Kingdom of God, and not to give us a definition of God. It is a drama of contrasts, between the actions of the master and the servant that should be the focus of our attention.

### An Impossible Debt

The servant owes his master ten thousand talents. This is an incomprehensible amount, like listening to an account of our national budget. One talent equaled six thousand denarii, which would mean sixty million denarii, or that the amount of the debt was over ten million dollars. The average worker's wage for a day's work was one denarius. This would mean that it would take a worker well over a hundred and fifty thousand years to pay off such a debt.

Now there are many reasons that can be given why our Lord used such a fantastic sum. It could be that Jesus was pointing out how great our debt is to God and how great is his mercy when compared to our debt to one another. Or it may be that Jesus is saying that great debts are easy to forgive because they are impossible to pay, but small debts are difficult to forgive because payment is a practical possibility.

One of my students tells about a doctor who lived in a small mill town in North Carolina. When he died almost every poor family in town owed him money. His wife discovered the accounts of these debts and went to court to collect them. After the judge had examined the records, he turned to the widow and said, "There isn't a court in the land that could force payment of these bills. For on each, in your husband's own handwriting, are the words, 'too poor to pay.' "

When a debt is impossible there is little else to do but forget it. Such an action doesn't require a forgiving heart. But when a debt is within the means of the one who owes it, that's another thing.

Jeremias[4] sees in the impossibility of the debt an appeal to our sense of what is right. If God forgives us so great and impossible a debt, how can we refuse to do the possible and forgive a fellow human being?

For me, the incomprehensible amount owed to the master is simply a dramatic device used by a skilled storyteller to heighten the theatrical properties of the plot. The great contrast between the two debts of the two main characters makes for a better story.

### More Than He Asked

Hearing that he with his wife and his children were to be sold into slavery, the servant falls on his knees and asks for time to pay off the debt. "Lord, have patience with me, and I will pay you everything." In spite of the impossible debt, the servant does not ask that it be canceled or forgotten. He simply asks for an extension — for an opportunity to try at least to pay it back. That is a positive point to his credit. The servant was not all bad. The master, however, was all good. He gives the debtor so much more than he asked for. The servant asked for an extension. The master gives him a cancellation. Such is the extent of God's forgiveness. He always gives us more than we asked for, and certainly more than we deserve. In fact, he gives us many, many times more than we could even have hoped for.

There is a popular song based on a mountain legend about a wild young man who, despite the fact that he was raised in a devout and religious home, ended up in prison. When his sentence was about up, he wrote home begging his mother's forgiveness for all the unhappiness he had caused in her life. He asked that if she could find it in her heart to forgive him, she was to tie a white cloth on the old oak tree in the front yard. That would be a sign that he was forgiven and welcome to come back home. As the bus made the familiar turn in the road, and his home came into view, the young man was torn with apprehension. He was afraid to look. When he finally mustered up the courage to open his eyes, the sight was breathtaking. Not only the old oak tree, but the house and the barn and the fences and everything standing were covered with strips of white cloth.

So with God. We ask for a little and we get a lot. We ask God to forgive our sins and he willingly goes to the cross and suffers not only for all our past sins but for all the sins we might yet commit. And more, he dies, not just to erase our wrongdoings, but to make us new men and women that we might be welcomed back into the father's house with open arms. We ask him to forgive us as sinners, and he makes of us saints. We ask, like the prodigal, for the lowest privilege of being a slave in our father's house, and he gives us the highest position of being his sons and daughters.

### Act Two

Act Two begins a drama of comparisons and contrasts. It is introduced by the phrase, "as he went out," which points out the immediacy of the action which follows. He meets a fellow servant who owes him one hundred denarii. At once two glaring contrasts emerge from the encounter.

The first contrast is that the difference between the two debts owed is glaring — sixty million over against one hundred denarii. Now it should be noted here that knowing students as I do and how they tend to exaggerate a good story when they hear one, the amount of contrast between the two debts undoubtedly grew each time the story was retold. But allowing for such storytellers' exaggerations, the vast differences between the two debts is an essential element in the story.

As the drama builds, the forgiven servant seizes his debtor by the throat and says, "Pay what you owe!" This action of seizing his friend by the throat is the second obvious contrast. In the first act we see a picture of dignity and compassion exercised by the king. In this second act we see uncontrolled passion and violence on the part of the recently forgiven servant.

The story goes on with the fellow servant falling down and beseeching him, "Have mercy on me and I will pay you." After two strong notes of contrast between the two incidents, we are confronted with a striking similarity. The words of the plea made by the second servant are the same words which the forgiven servant had used as he stood before the king. He had no excuse for forgetting what had just happened to him, because he was hearing his same words coming back to him. He was actually facing himself, and his own desperate need was being replayed in the need of his fellow servant. But he failed to see it.

Here is the irony of our shabby hero. He thought that the crisis of his life was that moment when he stood guilty before the king. In reality his moment of crisis stood before him in the person of his fellow servant begging him for mercy. If God is to be found anywhere in this parable, he is seen in the pleas of the servants and their desperate need. For as we do it unto the least of these my brethren, we do it unto the Lord. The king in our story encountered God in the plea of his slave for mercy, and the king did right before God. He served his God by forgiving his debtor. But the servant, when he encountered God in the plea of his fellow servant, turned his back upon God and refused him. This was the crisis point of his life, and he struck a deadly blow against himself.

In the light of this interpretation, the parable teaches by contrast the lesson that as we forgive others, we serve, praise and please the God who has so graciously forgiven us.

## Act Three

Act Three begins with judgment — not on the part of the king but by the friends of the unforgiving servant. The parable states that, "When his fellow servants saw what had taken place, they were greatly distressed." Now the use of this word, "distressed," suggests some interesting speculations. If they had been really concerned for the injured second servant, they would have, like the king, shown compassion. Since the debt that the second servant owed was small, they could have taken up a collection and paid the debt for him. However, the structure of the story demands that they react not with compassion and a quick practical solution, but that they act out of the realization that a serious injustice has occurred. This is important not only at this point in the story, but it becomes much more important as the story develops, for in the end they become the ones who punish the wicked servant. As we will point out later on, the king returns the unforgiving servant to them, and their attitude of anger is vital if the wicked servant is to get all that he deserves.

The servants who carried the story to the king are also important because they accentuate how obvious was the wrongness of the deed done by the unforgiving servant. This tells us that we know, without being told or taught, that it is wrong to fail to forgive others when we have experienced a fantastic forgiveness ourself. The unfairness of the wicked servant's actions was apparent even in the sight of the other servants. How much more must it be so in the sight of God?

When the lord in the parable hears what has taken place, he reflects the anger of the people by calling the unforgiving servant "wicked." He had expected that his mercy would have generated mercy in his servant, but it did not. The experience of fantastic forgiveness had not changed him. He was the same man as he was before. So the king delivers him over to the jailers.

The Greek word used here is **basanistaes**, better translated as "tormentors," which suggests not imprisonment in a jail but a kind of public punishment. The tormentors were more than likely the distressed people who had brought the story of the man's wicked behavior to the king. The implication is that the wicked servant is going to have to live with the daily reminder — in the form of his neighbors — of how terribly wrong his actions have been. His sentence of punishment is to be the constant reminder of his foul lack of forgiveness in the hopes that one day he will repent.

Here is a very positive point in the story. The main concern of the king is not the money owed, but the character of his servant. The king must have loved his servant dearly. He forgives him of his great debt. When the king hears how badly he treats his fellow servant, he turns him over to the people of the village with the hope that their constant reminder of his wickedness might do what the king's forgiveness has failed to do.— namely, make of him a kind and forgiving person.

Some people will not learn and be changed by the easy manner of kindness and compassion. They have to learn their lessons the hard way. Hard knocks are some times necessary to change the hardhearted.

The important thing is there is no justification for finding in this final act of the parable and its judgment pronounced by the king an image of hell and eternal punishment. For one thing, when we consider the two judgments which the king handed down, the second is far less stringent than the first. In the first instance (verse 25), the king ordered him to be sold as a slave with his wife and his children in order to pay the debt. In the second judgment, the king merely orders him to be thrown in jail, or as we have pointed out above, better translated, to be delivered over to his tormentors. The judgment in the first instance is far more severe than that of the second. If the idea of hell were intended as a threat for our lack of forgiveness, it would seem that the second judgment should have been far greater than the first.

The story would suggest that the action of the king,

sending the man to his tormentors, was not angry revenge or judgment on his part, but a continuation of his compassion toward his servant. He was doing for the man what the king thought was best. Mercy had failed to change the unforgiving servant so now he would have to learn the hard way.

And the parable adds, "So God will do to all of us." This is not so much a warning as it is a promise. It says that God is determined that we will be changed and become the persons he intends us to be, in this case, forgiving persons. God prefers to change us the gentle way with a fantastic experience of forgiveness. This he does on the cross. But if we refuse and turn our backs on this expression of his love and forgiveness, he will not give up but use whatever hard means necessary to change our hearts and make us into the new persons who can live in the Kingdom he has provided for us.

## Traditional Interpretations

Most scholars take a moralistic approach toward this Parable of the Unforgiving Servant. Their interpretations can be summarized under two major classifications.

## Obedience

The first is the idea of **obedience**. The actions of the king are identified with God's mercy and his judgment. The meaning which follows is clear. If we forgive, we will be forgiven. God's mercy and forgiveness are thereby conditional, depending upon our first forgiving others. The ultimate decisive issue, then, of the act of forgiveness is not what God does but what we do. Therefore, we do not need a savior to go to the cross for us; all we need to do is be a forgiving person worthy of God's forgiveness. This makes mockery of our Lord's words as he hangs on the cross, "Father, forgive them, for they know not what they do." If forgiveness demands obedience to the law — that we must forgive others — then we are not free from the law in Christ and we hear no gospel.

## Obligation

The second classification of interpretations is made up of those who stress the idea that because we are forgiven by God, we stand under an **obligation** to forgive others. This is a milder approach and places God in a far better light, but it is just as legalistic and morally binding on the listener as the **obedience** approach.

Now both of these classifications of interpretations are at best unsatisfactory. They are inconsistent with the gospel — the good news that salvation depends not on us, but is an act of free grace given to us by our Savior, Jesus Christ. For the **obedience** approach makes our forgiveness something we purchase with our own meritorious good deeds of forgiving others. The approach of **obligation** makes of God's forgiveness not good news of our forgiveness, but a debt which constantly hangs over our heads. We must pay this debt or God will foreclose on the mortgage of our forgiveness and take it away from us.

Neither approach is the good news of the gospel. For it is not good news that we have to buy our forgiveness, or are constantly in debt because of it. This would deny the basic necessity of the cross. For if forgiveness is something that must be bought or something demanding we spend the rest of our life paying for, then why a savior?

The central message of the cross is that we are unworthy of God's forgiveness. There is no merit we can achieve by our own efforts. Therefore Christ takes on our obligations and fulfills our obedience. As we stand before the judgment of God, we cling only to Christ our mediator and savior. It is his righteousness that is the basis of our forgiveness and not our forgiving nature or our impressive personal record of seventy-times-seven acts of forgiveness accomplished.

## Forgiveness Is a Happening

The moralistic approaches to this parable fail to comprehend the profound power that radiates from it. When, on the other hand, we look at this parable in and of itself as story, we see that its structure is simple and direct. It is about one man who had a fantastic thing happen to him. He is a tragic hero, however, because despite the drama of his experience, he is the same man at the end of the story as he was at the beginning. Much happens outside himself, but nothing really happens to him as a person.

This is a story of strong and dramatic words and actions — a man on his knees crying for mercy, the threat of slavery for him and his whole family, seizing a man by the throat and demanding, "pay me all you owe," and the king's words echoing down the corridors of the palace, "You wicked servant." These words are meant to penetrate into the very depths of our thinking and deposit there the burning questions of the very nature of a person, and what it means to be truly human before our God.

What we have here is not a nice little moral story about forgiveness, or a simple warning against our lack of forgiveness. We have something far more. We have a dramatic story revealing that forgiveness is a happening. Something radical happens to us when we are forgiven — truly forgiven. Forgiveness is not just something that happens **for** us; it is something that happens **to** us.

The key phrase of this parable is "from your heart." Christ says, "If you do not forgive your brother from your heart." The Greek word used here is **kardia** which is translated, "heart," but does not refer to the organ of the body we commonly call our heart. Rather it means the seat of the inner man. It means the control room within us where all our reactions originate. It includes the will, the emotions, and human reason. So, when Jesus admonishes us to forgive "from your hearts," then we are to forgive because of what we **are** at the very center of our being. Forgiveness is more than an act we do; it is a spontaneous expression of who we are.

The parable stresses the fact that when we meet God in a meaningful experience, we are changed by that experience and become different persons. As Christ said to Nicodemus, "You must be born again." If we are not changed, we have really not made contact with God. He has come to us, but we have moved out of his touch.

As we have stated above, the structure of the story points up the real tragedy that happens in the parable. It is the tragic account of a pathetic hero who was the same person at the end of the parable as he was at the beginning. He was unforgiving by nature. He experienced a fantastic act of forgiveness, but in the end he was the same old unforgiving man as before. He had not been reborn a new forgiving person.

We cannot experience forgiveness and remain the same. If we are unchanged, then we have had no real experience of forgiveness. This is true in all of life. We cannot go through a meaningful and moving experience without being affected by it. When we experience the death of a loved one, or the birth of our first child, or a serious family quarrel, or are betrayed by a friend, these experiences leave their mark upon us. This is what it means to be human. But the tragic hero of our story failed to measure up, and he was therefore less than human.

Legend tells us that when Leonardo DaVinci decided to paint the "Last Supper," he went out to find a model for the face of Christ. He found a successful, healthy, happy business man who had the perfect face. Several years later he needed a model for the face of Judas. He found him in the gutter in front of the local tavern. He was drunk, dirty and dying of consumption. Leonardo was shocked to discover that it was the same man who only a few years ago had posed for the face of Christ. The man's business had failed, his wife and children had left him and his best friends had forsaken him. He had been completely changed by one tragic circumstance and experience after another.

Now this legend is a striking illustration of the fact that experiences change people. And this is exactly what our Lord is stressing with his parable about the unforgiving servant. He is saying to his disciples and to us, "God has forgiven you and this is no insignificant event. This is an experience of major proportions intended to radically change you." To sit around and calculate how many times we should forgive our brother is a sure indication that we are the same narrow, self-centered person we were before we heard of God's forgiveness. If forgiveness does not work a change in us, we have never really experienced forgiveness. For an essential element of God's act of forgiveness is the gift of a forgiving heart beating in the breast of a new person. When God forgives us, he makes of us a forgiving person, not just a person who forgives a certain number of times.

So often we think that what we need when we approach God seeking forgiveness is the elimination of certain acts we have committed, like erasing a wrong chalk mark on a chalkboard. But God looks at forgiveness in a far different way. He sees forgiveness not as the erasing of a deed but the altering of the doer of the deed. He desires to change not what the person has done, but who the person is.

Remember in the story that the servant asked only for time — to postpone his debt. But the king gave him much more. He canceled all the debt. He closed the books. Now the man could start a new life, free from past burdens, because he was in a true sense a new man. By this our Lord wanted to expand our ideas and views of forgiveness, allowing us to see it not just as a pardon for certain offenses, but as an opportunity for a completely new life. Forgiveness thereby becomes not a cancellation of an old deed, but the creation of a new life.

God grieves when he sees the lack of forgiveness in our lives, not because we do not give back to him pound for pound what he has given us, but because our lack of forgiveness indicates that we are refusing his action of forgiveness in our lives. We are refusing to become the person

God so desperately desires us to be.

## The Gospel

Now the parable ends on a very tragic and somber note. The unforgiving servant is handed over to the tormentors and we are left in doubt as to the final outcome. But, thank God, though the parable ends on a note of tragedy and doubt, the Gospel does not end with this parable. The Gospel proclaims that the same Lord who told this parable to the disciples was the same Lord who faced the agony of Gethsemane and the nails of Golgotha. Here is the fantastic experience of forgiveness. Simple words spoken for the unworthy — spoken for you and for me: "Father, forgive them, for they know not what they do." This is God's final and last word on forgiveness. And it was spoken for us.

# 6

# God's Good News of Grace

**The Parable of the Workers in the Vineyard**
**Matthew 20:1-15**

This parable mentions familiar issues that we read about in our daily newspaper — unemployment, wages, and the struggle between labor and management. But when you hear this parable, it is obvious that it offers little help for our contemporary economic problems; any manager who treated his employees like this master did would be in immediate trouble with labor unions and would find himself with a major strike on his hands and a picket line of disgruntled laborers marching around his vineyard.

Many preachers have, however, tried to moralize this parable and use it as the basis for a sermon that grapples with the curse of unemployment. Charles W. F. Smith in his book, *The Jesus of the Parables,*[1] states that this approach does "violence" to the parable as "nothing could have been farther from Jesus' mind or purpose."

## Allegory

Historically, the parable has been treated by many interpreters as an allegory, and it does lend itself well to such efforts. Irenaeus, for example, sees the various calls to the workers as periods of history from creation to the end of time. The vineyard is righteousness, the householder, God, and the denarius is immortality. Origen follows the same pattern but calls the denarius "salvation." St. Augustine calls the denarius "life eternal." Since Julicher, however, allegory has been avoided by interpreters, who have been more concerned to find the theological point the parable is meant to convey. To do this it is necessary to first discover the setting of the parable. What were the circumstances that prompted Jesus to tell this particular parable?

### Riches in Heaven

Matthew places this parable after our Lord's encounter with the rich young ruler. The young man came seeking a way to eternal life. After they agreed that the commandments were to be kept, Jesus adds the stinger that the rich young man should go out and sell all that he has and give it to the poor. And he shall have riches in heaven. Now we know that this was too much for the young man. His eager excitement left him and he walked away downcast and disappointed. However, Peter, who overheard the conversation, had a much different reaction. Those words, "riches in heaven," sounded very good to the old fisherman. After all, he had given up his boats and his fishing business, and now his master was saying that when you give up everything you will have riches in heaven. Peter couldn't wait to get more details on this attractive promise.

"Look," he said to Christ, "we have left everything and have followed you. What will we have?" The answer Christ gives doesn't disappoint Peter. In fact it was more than he had expected. Christ not only promises him a hundred times more than he had given up, but he promises Peter would be a prince and sit on a throne. All this plus eternal life. However, Christ does not leave the matter there, but goes on to tell the parable of the Workers in the Vineyard which is meant to protect Peter from forming some wrong conclusions about the promised reward.

Oesterley[2] believes that Jesus added the parable because, even though he agreed with Peter that right doing deserves rewards, he didn't want the disciples to conclude from this that good works alone would be sufficient to attain salvation.

## Jealousy

Other scholars, notably Dodd[3] and Jeremias,[4] see this parable addressed not to Peter or the disciples but to the Jewish leaders in an effort to vindicate the gospel against its critics.

Mark and Luke, as well as Matthew, record the encounter with the rich young ruler and the question of Peter, including Christ's promise of reward, but only Matthew records the parable, placing it after Peter's question. In the light of this, Jeremias[5] takes the position that Mark and Luke show that Matthew does not reflect the original setting of the parable. We must therefore go behind Matthew and study the parable without reference to the setting. When we do, we discover that the parable does so much more than simply answer the question asked by Peter. If that had been its primary purpose, then why the second part where the workers complain about the unfair treatment?

It is precisely in the second part of the parable, according to the rule of "end stress," that the point of the parable is to be found. This episode pictures the workers who are "indignant, rebel and protest" and receive the humiliating reply, "Are you jealous because I am good?" The parable is clearly addressed to those who resembled the murmurers, those who criticized and opposed the good news, namely the Pharisees. Jesus intended to show them that the coming of the Kingdom turns previously held standards upside down. If people are to accept the Kingdom, they must be willing to radically change their way of thinking. What you considered wrong before is now right. That which was unworthy is now preferred. The outcasts become the insiders. The neglected now become the privileged.

Here, according to Jeremias,[6] we have recovered the true historical setting of the parable. We are suddenly transported into a concrete situation in the life of Jesus, such as the Gospels frequently depict. Over and over again we hear the charge brought against Jesus that he is the companion of the despised and the outcast. Repeatedly, Jesus is compelled to justify his conduct and to vindicate his good news to sinners. So in this parable, Jesus is saying that this is what God is like — so good, so full of compassion for the poor — how dare you revile him? We will have more to say about this interpretation later on.

## No Demands

Both of these interpretations — the one which holds the parable to be an answer to Peter, and the other which takes the position that the parable is a rebuttal of the Pharisees — agree at one central point, namely, that God rewards according to his own standards. Though we can expect reward for doing good, we can make no demands or claims upon God. Special favors will be granted, and we are not to calculate the actions of God or criticize his desire to give to the undeserving. We are not to evaluate the Kingdom by our old standards but are to embrace the new.

## The Joy of Work

The parable presents the Kingdom of God as a vineyard. This is not unusual, for it is a familiar image used in the Old Testament. However, to depict the Kingdom as a place where people work, might seem to be in contrast to the many other parables of Jesus where the Kingdom is a banquet where people relax, feast and enjoy themselves. Particularly is this true when people view work as a curse. Since the fall, work is often viewed as a state opposite to that of grace. After all, it was the curse of labor that accompanied the act of being driven out of the garden of paradise. The cool streams and quiet meadows of paradise have become the filthy factories and noisy streets of commerce. Work has become an unwelcome necessity. We have to work to live.

However, this activity we call work, when done as a means of self-expression without consideration of wage or pay, can be a source of joy. Ask the many unemployed who really want to work but cannot because of their age or limited abilities. Creative work can give meaning and value to living. It can be a desired end in and of itself. It can make a person feel needed and important.

It is true that in this day of assembly-line production, where men have to put in so many hours of activity with only one end in mind — the paycheck at the end of the week — work is the undesirable necessity. Most of us work, looking forward to the day when we can retire and start living. This seems to be the attitude of the men in our parable. Even though there were no assembly line factories, there were vineyards and cucumber fields where men sweated in the hot Palestinian sun, and labored until their muscles ached in order to earn enough to put dark bread and dry cheese on their tables. Then as now men were enslaved by an economic system, and work was a part of that unattractive process.

Thielicke[7] points out that this attitude toward work was the folly of the men in our parable and the beginning of their downfall and disappointment. They should have rejoiced in the opportunity which was theirs. Instead of being jealous of the last-hour workers getting an equal wage, they should have felt sorry for them that they had had so little time to enjoy working in the vineyard of the master. Now this may sound unreasonable to the factory worker of today, but when you remember that the vineyard is an image of the Kingdom of God, then work takes on a different status. It is work in the best sense of the word. It is the work we were intended to do and therefore a work of self-expression and creativity.

Lindemann[8] points out that the issue is not the length or the amount of the labor, but the spirit in which one enters into work. The joy of working is really the great reward the householder gives and not the wage at the end of the day. The wage is necessary to eat, but the work gives meaning and purpose to life. In the light of this, there is no great contrast between a vineyard and a banquet as we might at first have thought, for both can be an opportunity for an experience of joy. If the vineyard is the Kingdom of God, then work is a privilege, for it is that for which we were created. Work is a desirable activity, for it is to serve with and for the Lord our God.

## Authority

Many interpreters see this parable as basically a teaching concerning the nature of God's ultimate authority as ruler and redeemer.

God is first of all an absolute master. He does, the parable tells us, what he desires to do with what is his. The Kingdom of God is no democracy where we decide by a majority vote the way things will be done. The Pharisees had forgotten this. Their privileged position among the Jews had gone to their heads and hardened their hearts. They had done their duty before God and they had done it well, better than any other men. This put them in a position above the rank and file where they could speak on behalf of God, for they had seniority in the vineyard of God's workers. In their eyes this upstart from Nazareth hadn't even paid his union dues, yet already he was taking charge as if his father owned the place. But what was even more distasteful and distressing to the Pharisees was the way tax collectors, sinners and women of the streets were getting preferred treatment before them. From the viewpoint of the Pharisees, Jesus was flinging open the gates of God's vineyard-kingdom to the scum of Jerusalem. Where was there justice in this? This could not be the will of God because it went contrary to everything the

Pharisees knew was right. So they challenged Jesus on the spot.

Jesus met them head on. He said in effect, "You are good men. Right? Everybody knows this and respects you for it. That is the wage you bargained for. That is what God gives you. As for these others, the sinners and the poor, they have their own unique relationship with God. He will do with them as he wants, for you are all only workers in his vineyard. And of this vineyard God is master. He has absolute authority to establish wages and pay rewards according to his will and his will alone."

Now this is a hard statement for us to take, particularly because we live in a democracy built on the principle that total power corrupts. Because of this, no one person should have unlimited power. This is a sound principle built upon the Biblical truth that all men are sinners, and therefore we must have restrictions and balances of power to protect society from dictatorship and tyranny. But, you see, Jesus in our parable is not talking about sinful man and his use of power, but God and his use of power. Power is an element of God's goodness. The failure to acknowledge this absolute power of God is the source of most of our problems. We work and fret as if everything depended upon us, the strength of our hands, the brilliancy of our minds, and cleverness of our wits. It is only natural that when we start to think about salvation we look immediately for the price tag — the work order — asking, "What must we do to accomplish this thing?" And in most cases we place the emphasis not on the word "do," where it belongs, but on "we," because we are convinced that we have something worthwhile to contribute to any enterprise that is going to succeed. After all, "You don't get something for nothing," and God needs our help to get his job done — at least if it's going to be done right.

This lack of acknowledging God's authority is glaringly apparent in our churches today. We give God a polite salute in the affairs of the church, but little else. We begin our meetings with prayer and ask for his help and guidance, and then proceed as if God did not exist. We make up our minds on decisive issues following our own whims, tastes and desires, and in many cases, prejudices. When we are confronted with decisions such as calling a pastor, building a new church, or remodeling an old one, when we face matters of stewardship or evangelism, when we are confronted by liturgical changes, we make these decisions on the basis of what we can afford, or how we feel about it, or what we think, what we want, or what we desire.

It is this kind of self-centered assumptive take-over of the management of God's vineyard that our parable speaks to. For here we collide head on with the absolute sovereignty of God. He is the master of the vineyard, and his will alone decides what is going to be done with what is his.

### Generous Master

However, we rejoice in the sovereignty of God and in his absolute power, for though he is master, he is a most generous and kind master. Here the parable does a magnificent job of blending power with grace, and judgment with redemption. God asserts his authority. He denies us the right to lay claim on his redemptive activity, but he lays claim on us and freely gives us what we cannot accomplish for ourselves.

There is a legend which tells of a young boy whose mother was ill. Knowing how much she loved flowers, the boy went to his room and there in the top drawer of his chest was his meager savings. It was just a few pennies but it represented all his worldly wealth. He took it and headed for the village market to buy some flowers for his mother. When he arrived, he found that there was not a flower left for sale. Walking home bitterly disappointed, he passed a magnificent garden. Acres of glorious roses were in full bloom. He asked the man tending the garden if he might buy one. The gardener told him he was sorry but these were the royal gardens. The roses belonged to the king and were not for sale. The little boy turned away in tears, for this was his last hope.

Then a voice called to him. It was the young prince of the realm. "The gardener is right," he said, "these are the royal gardens. The flowers belong to my father the king and he does not sell them, but he does give them away." And with this the prince picked an armful of the most beautiful roses in the gardens and placed them in the delighted arms of the little boy.

So with God and his Kingdom. Membership in his Kingdom is not for sale at any price but it is given freely by the kind mercy of God. Therefore, do not grumble at his illogical generosity to others, for what they receive is a gift and what we receive is also a gift; for it is far more than we could ever have earned for ourselves.

### Tragic Justice

The tragic note of the parable is that the all-day workers were so concerned with justice for themselves that they failed to experience something far greater than justice, namely, the mercy of their master to those in need. They missed the joy of seeing the generosity of God at work.

How often we fail to see the fullness of God operative in the lives of others because we are so concerned with a fair share of justice for ourselves.

It is like the two little children I saw at the Christmas parade last year. They were arguing and fighting about whose turn it was to sit on their father's shoulders to better see the parade. It turned out that they failed to see any of the parade because they were afraid one was going to get more than his fair share of their father's shoulders.

So with us. We miss and waste so much of the joys of life because of petty jealousy and the fear that someone else is getting more than we.

The great Russian writer Dostoyevsky tells the story of a woman who found herself in hell and felt she did not belong there. She could not bear the suffering and cried out in agony for the mercy of God. God listened and was moved with pity. "If you can remember one good deed that you did in your lifetime, I will help you," said God. Wracking her brain, she remembered that once she had given a starving neighbor an onion. God produced the onion complete with stem. The woman grabbed the onion, and God began to pull her up and out of hell. But others, damned with her, began to grab hold of the woman's skirts to be lifted out, too. The stem of the onion held and would have saved them all, but the woman began to kick and scream for them to let go. Thrashing about trying to dislodge her friends was too much for the onion and the stem snapped, plunging them all back into the depths of hell.

So with us, holding on to our onion stems, our denarii of good works, we lash out jealously at those who have not done as much as we have for God. It is the irony of self-righteousness that the very good works we thought might get us into heaven often prove to be that which drops us from grace into the fires of hell.

There is no bargaining table between ourselves and God — only a communion table where everyone comes and kneels at the same height before God. All of us are equal, for we are all sinners and unworthy of the feast. If by chance we think that we are a little better than the one kneeling beside us, then when the elements are passed we will receive not the body and blood of Christ but only bread and wine.

## God of the Unexpected

Luther[9] points out that this parable presents the unexpected contrast between the economy of this world and the economy of the Kingdom. We live in a fallen world where we experience an economy determined by sinful necessity. So much work equals so much pay and overtime is rewarded with bonuses.

In the parable, God's Kingdom stands in direct contrast. Here, people receive according to their needs rather than their deeds. They get so much more than they earn or deserve. The problem is that we live in both worlds, and when we apply the economy of the Kingdom to our world we find ourselves faced with great difficulties, especially when we demand wages without work or expect worldly masters to give us something for nothing.

The only answer, according to Luther, is that in this world we should, as good Christians, accept and abide by its standards of economy. We should expect no special privileges or treatment. We should work our fair share for honest wages. When we find ourselves in positions of management, we should reward superior labor and not pay people for their idleness.

It is evident that Luther had not yet encountered the massive power of labor unions which have created their own kingdom, but what Luther does go on to say makes good sense. He says that we should accept the economy of this world, but at the same time practice when and where we can, in our personal lives, the economy of the Kingdom of God. When the opportunity presents itself, we are to practice graciousness and give to the undeserving, the needy, the helpless, and the unemployed. We cannot by our own strength expect to change the world and force the strong to serve the weak, but we can witness within this world of the Kingdom, where the greatest are servants. We may not reform the world and bring it to its knees with towel in hand, but we can at least reveal and testify by our actions to a kingdom where the master washes the feet of the lowly. By so doing we will show the world that there is a better way. Thus, we become a foretaste of the new world which is to come.

### Radical Judgment

Edmund Steimle[10] points out that this parable is meant to startle us by presenting "an entirely different way of looking at things — with God's way of looking at things. There is," adds Steimle, "a radical difference . . . between our way of judging people and God's."

We judge horizontally. God's judgment is vertical. The major issue is not what a man actually accomplishes in relation to, or in comparison with others, but what are the inner motivations that cause a person to act. God's concern is here. He looks at why we do what we do.

God also, the parable suggests, judges according to opportunity. The latecomers were idle most of the day, not because they were lazy or refused to work, but because no one would hire them. Many in our world are burdened with handicaps. People born in slums are denied education because of poverty or race. Some are ugly, or weak, or crippled. People are not born equal, therefore they should not be equally judged. Many may have good intentions and good motivations but no opportunity. God, therefore, recognizes this and judges according to opportunity as well as need. The parable thereby teaches that the Kingdom is ruled not by unbending law but by unending grace and mercy.

### The Great Surprise

From all that has been said thus far concerning this parable, it is obvious that there will be many surprises for us as we encounter more and more of the Kingdom of God. We will experience an economy and a justice similar and yet so very different from anything we have known in this world. For God is bound not by rules or laws but by mercy and love. Some will labor long, others briefly in the vineyard, and this will not go unnoticed by God. But when the judgment comes, we will find that the last will be treated like the first because the last are in need of grace as much as the first. There is no way we can fully understand this, for we are looking through this parable into the heart of God, and there love burns so brightly that human eyes are blinded by its brilliance.

Who then can grumble? The truth of the parable silences all criticism by proclaiming to us that the worst receive more from God than even the best deserve. No one can measure up to the demands and cost of God's grace. Nothing we do can begin to earn the wage God so freely gives. Only a cross on a forsaken hill, and a young man betrayed and innocently beaten can be singled out as a good day's work before God. Whatever we get, we do not deserve. Therefore we do not complain but rejoice, for in the Kingdom of God even the worst receive more from God than the best deserve.

There was once a man who saved string. He died. When his daughter came to sort out his personal belongings so that the house could be sold, she found several large balls of string which the old man had saved through the years. This did not surprise her, but then while cleaning out a drawer she found a little box. On it there was a label which read, "Pieces of string too short to save." How do you react to such a story? Do you cry or do you laugh? What incongruity —even absurdity. He saved string that was too short to save. Yet is this not the incongruity and absurdity of the gospel Christ came to proclaim? God saves that which is too short to save, that should not be saved. Yet this is the glory of the gospel. It is not the result of our logical thinking, but of the loving thinking of God. The parable points out to us that because God is love and Christ is savior, no human life is too insignificant or no service in the Kingdom is too short to be judged by God unworthy of salvation.

## A Fair Contract or Generous Grace

Finally, the true meaning of the parable comes through when it is looked at apart from its setting and context. As a story with its own integrity, it presents the two basic relationships we can have with God, namely law or trust.

The structure of the parable creates a drama of balance between a relationship created by the law and a relationship created by trust. There are two classes of workers that dominate the story. The first group of workers enters into a bargain, a contract, an agreement with the master of the vineyard before it starts to work. The work and the wage are agreed upon. If you do the work, you get the wage. This group represents the relationship of the law. If you fulfill the law, you are rewarded with salvation.

The ones hired last form the second group of workers. They make no bargain, possess no contract; they are simply standing in the marketplace waiting. The owner sends them into his vineyard with the directive, "Well then, go to work in the vineyard." They have no idea of what the wage will be if any at all. They go to the vineyard on pure faith. Therefore, they represent the relationship of trust. They trust the owner and that is the only agreement that exists between them and the owner.

Now between these two groups there is a third group which goes to work only with the promise of a fair wage. These persons are placed in the story because of dramatic necessity. In the structure of the story, they fulfill the literary need of a transition between the two extremes. They are not mentioned in the final accounting but give way to highlight the two extremes. At the one extreme you have those who go to work with a legal contract. At the other extreme you have those who go to work with nothing except the word of the master and their trust in him.

Knowing the continual conflict Christ had with the Jewish leaders, the meaning of the parable becomes clear. The Pharisees were contract lawyers to the "nth" degree. They knew the law and all its ramifications. For them, the only relationship that could possibly exist with God was a written contract agreed upon by both parties. They wanted the terms of relationship spelled out, written down, signed and sealed.

Christ says in this parable, "No, this is not the only way. There is another." It is important to note that the parable does not deny the validity of this contractual relationship with God that the law represents, but the parable suggests that this is not the only way. In Christ a new option is opened up, the option of grace and trust. It is a relationship expressed in his favorite image of God as Father. We work in the Kingdom-vineyard as a family, knowing and trusting that our father will provide abundantly for all our needs. We demand no contract or written agreement, only our father's word of invitation, "Come work in my vineyard."

This interpretation is strengthened when we compare this parable to a familiar rabbinic parable which serves as a model for the parable Jesus told. The rabbinic parable stands in direct contrast. It is about a laborer who was such a good and hard worker that the king removed him from the vineyard after only two hours' work, paid him a full day's pay and then went with him for a leisurely walk. To the other workers the king justified his actions by saying, "This man has done more in two hours than you have done in the whole day."

The change which Jesus makes in the parable vividly points up the meaning he was putting forth in his telling of the parable. With the genius of a master storyteller, he changes the climax of the story from the hard worker who gets the bonus to the underprivileged unemployed worker who finally gets his chance to share in God's vineyard. It is the good news that God has come to the lost — the unemployed, the outsider, to the poor, to the neglected — to all those who previously had no chance or opportunity. This new view of the Kingdom the Pharisees could not understand. So Jesus tells this parable in an attempt to open their eyes to the glorious good news about God and his mercy. God is good, gracious and generous; therefore, we are to place our trust in him and not in our own ability to work hard and long. We are not to draw up legalistic contracts with God, but simply trust him. For one greater than Moses and the Law has come among us, and he is Jesus Christ our Lord. Therefore, in the words of Wesley's hymn, let us "cast our crown before him," not mindful or jealous that others do less than we or have shorter service in his Kingdom. But in the knowledge of God's goodness, grace and generosity be "lost in wonder, love and praise." Once more, free grace has triumphed.

## 7

# Man's Deadly Desire to Play God

**The Parable of the Wicked Tenants**
**Matthew 21:33-46**
**Mark 12:9-19**
**Luke 20:9-19**

It is often surprising and sometimes shocking how much violence there is in Holy Scriptures. Our parable is a case in point. It has all the ingredients of a current movie — greed, robbery, beatings, stoning and murder.

When the Pharisees first heard this story, they were extremely upset and took angry offense at what they heard. Not that they were shocked with the violence of the story, for they had done their fair share of stoning sinners, and were the first to shout, "Crucify him," when blasphemy against God was evident. No, they were disturbed because they thought the point of the parable was aimed directly at them.

And the priests had the same reaction. Up to this time the scribes and the Pharisees had been the main target of Jesus' attack against Jewish leadership. Now the priests felt they were also becoming the target of Jesus' very pointed remarks.

Most scholars agree that this is the last parable Jesus told. Perhaps this is due to the fact that this story marks the point in the career of our Lord where his enemies firmly united themselves against him. The record reports, "The Scribes and chief priests tried to lay hands on him at that very hour." Now all the top level Jewish brass were in agreement. This upstart of a prophet from Nazareth must be silenced and silenced forever.

Interpreters faced with this parable are like the religious leaders of the Jews, frequently disturbed by the Parable of the Wicked Tenants. It is not the violence involved but the warning they themselves have given about the danger of allegorizing parables. And this story seems to cry out to be treated as an allegory. They recognize that many of the words used in the parable occur in Isaiah's Song of the Vineyard (Isaiah 5:1-7). Here the prophet uses the familiar image of Israel as God's vineyard as he pronounces judgment on God's people for not having yielded the proper fruits. This would suggest allegory as the proper interpretation of the Parable of the Wicked Tenants.

A. M. Hunter[1] tries to get around this dilemma by taking the position that this story is at the same time a parable with a point and an allegory. As allegory it is a presentation of the treatment the prophets receive as they come from God. It is also allegory in that it pictures the sending of God's son as God's last effort to win the love and obedience of his people. As a parable with a point, it is a word of hope that God is patient with his people and will give them yet another chance.

With this parable Christ is saying that the past does not always have to determine the future and the present. Many people hold that history repeats itself and human nature never changes. Because of this we are absolutely determined by our past. Study the past and you will be able to predict how man will react in similar situations today. This is the basis of tests, surveys and polls of human behavior. There is a pattern to be found, and once it is established it is a reliable basis for predictions of future actions. Variations and exceptions are acknowledged, but on the whole, we are determined by our past history and there is very little that we can do about it. We cannot change human nature, or reverse the direction of human history.

This parable, however, presents us with a picture of a landlord who acts as if his servants will change and react differently if only given a chance. Three times he sends his representatives to the tenants hoping they will eventually respond in a favorable way. He even takes the final and desperate step of sending his son. Certainly the tenants will be impressed by this action and react differently.

If Christ is the author of this parable, then it would seem that he is denying the rule that the past totally determines the future. And this would agree with the theology of the cross which states that we are freed from the sins of our past by the act of Christ taking to himself the sins of all. Now we are changed. We possess a new life — a different nature — a redeemed nature, enabled to surrender to God and follow his will. The rejection of God may have been the habitual pattern of humankind's relationship to God in the past. But now this legacy is broken by Christ and his cross, and we are given the power to break the habit of our sins and live in a new and obedient life.

### God as Enemy

Wallace[2] takes a rather unusual approach to the parable and sees in the actions of the Wicked Tenants a picture of our basic hatred of God. We resent God because he is God and we are only humans. The source of true sinfulness is our desire to be God. It is not so much the love of ourselves, but our uncontrollable ambition to be God that drives us forth to do the wicked deeds that mark our tragic history. God is therefore our enemy and we have declared war on him. For example, the motivation behind the crucifixion, according to Wallace, was not the blasphemy of a man claiming to be God when he was not. Rather, it was the unconscious fear in the hearts of the Jewish leaders that he might just be what he claimed. Men killed Christ not because they doubted his claims, but because they were beginning to believe them.

When a man claims to be God, the general reaction is to laugh at him and call him mad. But when we reach the point where we think he might be what he claims, then we take him seriously, and when we do, there are only two options open to us, either surrender to him, or reject and kill him.

Like the tenants in the vineyard, we do not like our master to come and interfere in our world. We have lived and worked here so long we think we own the world. Masters are best tolerated when they stay away and let their servants do the work. And gods are best worshiped when they do not meddle in the affairs of men, except where they are specifically needed. We want a God that can be manipulated to our own ends and become our servant rather than we, his. That is why people have preferred many gods rather than one. For with many gods there is a balance of power and they see to it that each god stays in his respective place.

The God of the Bible will not be controlled so easily as we might desire. He is aggressive and determined. When man refuses to hear him and lives as if he didn't exist, God becomes incarnate in human flesh. Now the existence of God cannot be denied. For God is present to sight and touch. At first man is surprised and refuses to believe his own eyes. But when he is convinced that God is truly present in the flesh, man does not fall down before him in fear. Rather, he realizes that God, having become man, is not vulnerable to man. So, seizing the opportunity to rid the world of God forever, man nails him to a tree of death. The bitter irony of it all. In a garden paradise it was under a garden tree that man suffered defeat and was driven out of God's perfect world. Now man tries by a tree to drive God out of man's imperfect world.

The point of the parable, according to Wallace, is the revelation that God places himself in this vulnerable position so that we can discover the hidden hatred we have for God. The cross permits our hatred to come out into the open so that we can face it and deal with it.

Archie Bunker sits in his chair, yells for a beer as he lashes out at all minorities. Now we can laugh at his ignoble character until suddenly we come to the realization that we are laughing at ourselves, and then it's not so funny. It is the kind of comedy that makes us cry. For Archie is the prototype of our own prejudices and little-mindedness.

So God permits himself to be nailed to a tree in order that we can stand face to face with all the hidden hatred that festers within us and cripples and corrupts our personhood. It is at this cross that we face our naked guilt and wickedness. And it is God's hope that once we see ourselves for what we really are, the sight will be so appalling and shocking that we will break before its vision and fall down on our knees crying out with Peter, "Depart from me, for I am a sinful man."

### The Progressive Process of Evil

When interpreters place the focus of attention on the people who tenant the land and how they react, we see not only, as Wallace has pointed out, our hidden hatred of God, but we are at the same time given a picture of the progressive process of evil.

There are three progressive steps to this pattern of evil's development in the parable. First, three slaves are sent to the tenants of the vineyard. According to Matthew, one is beaten, another stoned, and the third is killed. Secondly, the master sends other slaves. And the point is carefully made, ". . . more than the first time." Last of all, the master sends his own son. The conclusion drawn from this pattern is that each envoy is more and more impressive and their corresponding reception is increasingly violent. So it is with our acts of wrongdoing. Our rejection of God and his will for our lives is a step-by-step progression from bad to worse. The first time we lie, or cheat, or hate, or steal, it is a little action done with hesitation and a sense of guilt. The second time it is easier. There is no hesitation, some reservation, and only a little bit of guilt. The third time it's a cinch, and before you know it, wrongdoing becomes a way of life.

This is the dangerous pattern of alcoholism and drug addiction. The famous last words of the alcoholic are, "I can take just one drink." So in our parable evil and wrongdoing are habit-forming.

The progressive process of evil in our parable is seen also in the fact that the vine tenders start out as renters who desire only to share in the profits. Then they become profiteers who want to take all the goodies for themselves. And finally, in the end, they will be satisfied only when they have stolen the whole property for their own. Evil feeds upon itself. It is a developed habit which progressively grows from bad to worse.

Dan Otto Via sees in this parable the image of man, who "tries to possess as much as he possibly can regardless of the cost to others and as a result brings about his own destruction."[3] Then Via adds to the progressive process of evil the ultimate outcome, which is a picture of man who can no longer believe "there is a transcendent reality which undergirds him and fills his emptiness."[4] This is secular man who can no longer believe in God. Without such a power to restrain him, man turns to violence, both against humankind and nature. The inevitable result is that he does violence to himself.

## Absurd Expectation

As we look at the vine tenders there is the absurd expectation that they could acquire the property by murdering the heir. Most interpreters claim that there is no basis for this conclusion. It was stupid of them to think that they could win in the end and gain the property for themselves.

This illustrates the foolishness of wrongdoing. It was not just that these men were immoral and wicked, they were also stupid. Their efforts were so fruitless. And this illustrates the ultimate foolishness of all efforts to go against the will of God. Movies and novels often picture evil as cunning and clever. They take a romantic view of wickedness and create characters like Bonnie and Clyde who have a great fling of careless, carefree fun. Overlooking the outcome, we become fascinated by the glamour and excitement of the adventure and secretly envy their temporary escape from boredom. Even the tenants in our parable might appear to some as rebels to be admired for taking up arms against an unfair feudal society. But the fact cannot be avoided that what they did was foolish when you consider that their efforts were bound to fail.

## Another View

In his *Companion to the New Testament*, Harvey[5] takes the position that the actions of the tenants were not altogether foolish. In his view they had a legitimate basis for believing that they might get by with stealing the property of their master. He retells the parable as if it were based on an actual incident that might have happened in the days of our Lord.

According to his account, after the vineyard was rented to the tenants, they proceeded to grow vegetables in between the grapes with the idea of selling the vegetables, part of which profit would be their wage for tending the owner's grapes. In the meantime, the owner left town for a vacation, for there was nothing to do until the grapes were ready for harvesting, and that would take about four years.

During the first three years the owner sent only his servants to collect his small share of the profits from the vegetable crop. However, in the four years it was essential that the owner return, for this was the time of the first fruits and ritual regulations demanded his presence. However, this man faced a problem. Since he had received no rent, he had nothing but the title deed to prove his ownership of the vineyard. And since his servants had all been killed trying to collect the rent, there were no witnesses to prove that he had ever attempted to collect the rent. Now under Jewish law, according to Harvey, three years' undisputed possession of a piece of land enabled a person to claim ownership of that land over the holder of a deed.

The owner was in a very weak bargaining position with his tenants. Either he had to come himself or send his son. The tenants, on the other hand, thought that they had a very strong case for ownership on the basis of a neglected vineyard. Besides, they could have reasoned that since the owner had sent his son, and they had killed him, now the owner might just give it all up as a bad deal. After all, the owner might have thought that since he had no heir who would benefit from the investment, the vineyard just wasn't worth all the trouble it had cost him.

Then comes the dramatic climax of the story. The tenants miscalculated. The owner unexpectedly returned with a strong company of hired henchmen and threw all the wicked tenants into jail. So, even though the tenants failed in the end, their actions were not foolish. Like many businessmen of our day, they took a risk and lost. They had miscalculated the determination of the owner to claim and hold on to what was his.

If Harvey's reconstruction of a true situation was a possible basis for Jesus' parable, then the point of the parable would seem to be — don't underestimate the concern of God for what is his. And do not underestimate his revenge against those who rebel against him. The positive note of this interpretation is God's willingness to go to any lengths to claim what is his, namely our world and us. The negative note would be the lengths a person is willing to go to rebel against God and the inevitable condemnation which follows such actions.

## Kingdom Taken Away

Smith believes it to be an actual parable which has been "overlaid with allegorical modifications in the course of transmission and in the lights of events."[6] According to

Smith those who first listened to the parable would never have thought to apply the "killed son" to Jesus. This was before the crucifixion, and even the disciples failed to accept a violent death as the final outcome of Jesus' ministry.

Smith believes that the point of the parable is, "Due returns of an investment are called for and met in each successive case by deliberate refusal, accompanied by increased violence."[7] When the series of refusals do not call down punishment on their heads by the owner of the vineyard, they begin to feel secure. Security leads the tenants to believe that they really own the vineyard. The tenants' wickedness is therefore twofold. They keep the profits for their own, and they claim the property as their own.

The principle of "how much more" applies here. If this is the reaction of an earthly owner to rebellion, how much more will it be true of God as he grants stewardship to a chosen people? The conclusion is obvious. When we appropriate to our own private use what belongs to another, we must lose all rights and privileges of being stewards.

It is not unimportant that this parable is followed in Mark and Luke by the account of the tribute money. "Render unto Caesar the things that are Caesar's and to God the things that belong to God." The vineyard is God's and the fruits it produces are also God's. Anyone who forgets this and attempts to claim God's vineyard for his own and its resulting fruits as his personal profit stands in direct rebellion against the true owner of the vineyard.

This parable is not Jesus claiming his messiahship, but it is Jesus' claim that God is the owner of the vineyard and not the leaders of the Jews — the representative of Judaism. The important point Jesus is making with the parable is not the warning that you will kill the Son of God, but that the Kingdom will be taken away from you and given to others. This makes of the story not an allegory of what the Jews did to the prophets and the Son of God, but a parable warning the Jewish leaders that their claim to the Kingdom was to be given over to others because of their failure to produce a profit for the Lord. The parable presented the Jews with the question, "Who is Israel?" And the answer the parable gives is, "Those who produce fruits for the Lord."

The ultimate issue of our relationship to the Kingdom is, "Are we as good stewards producing fruits for the Lord?" The very task of the church is dramatically presented here. The church is not an end in and of itself, but a means. The church exists for the purpose of producing fruits for the Lord and the means through which God intends to call all people unto himself. The church is not to be identified as the Kingdom but as the instrument and means by which humankind is brought to and enters into the Kingdom of God.

## The Cost of Prophecy

Granskou's opinion is that the original version of the parable is to be found in the Gospel of Thomas. He believes the point made here is simply that the "people of God often treat messengers from God with shame and anger."[8] Therefore we should be alert and not reject or mistreat those who bring truth from God.

It could be added that since we are messengers of God we should expect rough treatment. Anyone who challenges the established order runs the risk of being beaten, treated shamefully, wounded, cast out, and sometimes killed. For so men have always treated the prophets.

Rodin has two statues. One is entitled **God** and he other **The Devil**. One shows a great hand and man's body resting peacefully in it. The first reaction is that certainly this is the statue of God, but Rodin has entitled it **The Devil**. The hand of God, in contrast, is tense. The grip is harsh and the body of man struggles within it. So we who are touched by the hand of God and called to be his prophets in this world should expect no easy way.

## The Divine Trap

Thielicke[9] is impressed by the improbability of the parable and asks where you would find an owner or a landlord who would allow his tenants to treat him so. But Thielicke believes this distortion to be intentional, for it shows God's incomprehensible concern for us. God's faithfulness is greater than our folly. The parable is for Thielicke a story of "divine initiative."

Other scholars have seen the same improbability and have even gone so far as to call it an absurdity. No vineyard owner would continue to send his servants into a growingly dangerous situation, and certainly not his own son. However, when the parable is applied to the "how much more" principle, then the absurdity dramatically points up the fact that God is more concerned for his people than for his property. Faced not with the problem of his loss of land but of his people, God is desperately determined to redeem and save them without destroying their freedom to rebel against him in the process. At the first evidence of rebellion, God could have come suddenly and destroyed his wicked and disobedient children. But he does not. He withholds his vengeful hand again and again, because he does not want to change his people at the expense of their freedom to be obedient to him.

His final effort is the most amazing bit of strategy. God uses our rebellion as the very means of our redemption. We create a cross to kill his son, and he uses that very instrument of death as the redemptive means of our salvation. The cross thereby becomes the divine trap. In our attempt to run away from God, we run directly into his arms nailed open on a cross, and from these arms of aggressive determined love there is no escape.

What might appear at first to be an improbable and absurd action becomes the wisdom of irresistible love. What appears to be God's weakness becomes God's greatest strength. God wins at the point of his apparently greatest failure. While we rejoice at our human victory over God, we suddenly discover that he has captured us and is the true victor. This is the mystery of the cross. We think we are killing God's son and claiming for ourselves a Kingdom of this world when in reality we are walking into the divine trap of love that flings open the gates of the Kingdom of God where sinners might enter in as saints.

## To Play God

When the parable is viewed apart from its setting, in and of itself, we find it is basically a story about foolish tenants. The plot poses the question of what happens when tenants attempt to be owners. And the answer it gives is that they bring down destruction upon themselves. The very land on which they stand and attempt so desperately to own is taken away from them.

The owner provides the conflict in the drama. His determination to get rent from his land creates the opportunity for the servants to oppose his attempts. The three visits of the messengers are meant to dramatize the change in attitude of the tenants and their growing desire to own the land for themselves. Each visit moves to the final extreme action of killing the owner's son which is the climax of their desire to be owners rather than just tenants of the land.

Then Jesus asks, "What then will the owner do to the tenants?" And the answer given is that he will kill them and turn his vineyard over to other tenants. The temptation here is to allegorize and see the owner as God and the fate of the wicked tenants the result of God's judgment. However, when we view the parable as parable and not as allegory, the owner's role in the story is simply to provide the dramatic climax of the tenants losing all claim to the land and being destroyed in the process.

Seen in this light the tenants bring down inevitable judgment upon themselves. Not that God judges them and finds them guilty, but that the very nature of their actions — stealing the land and making it their own — has the inevitable consequences of losing what they have and destroying them in the process.

As parable, this is not a story about God's judgment on our actions but a picture of how we act in God's creation where we are only tenants. When we try to be what we are not, when we take over the role of owner, when we play God, it is structured into the very nature of existence that we will be destroyed in the process.

When Jesus says, "The very stone which the builders rejected as worthless, turned out to be the most important stone," what he is saying is that the builders thought that the stone was worthless. But their judgment of it did not make it so. The tenants in the parable judged themselves to be owners, but that did not make it so. Things are what they are. They are what God created and intended them to be, and we cannot make it otherwise. We may not be happy just to be human and live in a world which is not our own. We may attempt to play God and take over the world, but when we do, we only judge and destroy others.

It is so easy to resign our responsibility and view God as a judge or an unbending landlord who passes harsh judgment and dishes out strong punishments upon all those who oppose him and rebel against him. It is much more evident of mature faith to realize we bring on ourselves judgment and punishment. God has created life in a certain pattern; he has structured creation and has ordained for us a particular destiny. When we disrupt this pattern, challenge this structure, or attempt to change our destiny, we are losers. If we don't eat, we starve to death. If we jump off a twenty-story building, life is crushed from us. If we touch fire, we are burned. This is not God's judgment. This is the way it is in the world God has created. So Jesus in this parable is telling it "like it is."

Now what does this say to us? First, it calls us to evaluate our stewardship. Are we really good tenants in the vineyard of the Lord? Just what kind of job are we doing with the responsible task God has given us — to serve him in the process of blessing all the nations of the world with the gospel of his good grace?

But perhaps more directly and pointedly it calls us to examine ourselves. Are we reversing the established roles of divine and human? Are we trying to become owners rather than tenants of this world? Are we trying to play God? Our vineyard — the world — is rich in natural resources. Are we playing God with ecology? Are we raping the earth of its energy? Are we killing its innocent creatures in our jungles and forests? Are we using the underdeveloped nations in the world to selfishly maintain our own high standard of living? These are the big questions, and Christ gives us a big answer that is difficult to avoid or get around. When we play God, when we forget we are tenants of this world and not owners, we are in trouble. For we can never succeed in our ambition to be owners; we can only lose our privilege of being tenants.

And the implications of this parable reach down into the more personal issues of our everyday life. Are we trying to play God with our children, our wives and husbands, our friends and associates? Are we living as if we can do anything we want with what we have and what is under our immediate control? Are we trying to play God in the lives of others?

The problem is an old one. Adam fell because he wanted to play God, and the roads of history are littered with the broken and fallen lives of men and women who have foolishly speculated that they could win at this game of playing God. We never seem to learn the direct teaching of this parable of the tenants — that God will tolerate just about anything except our devilish attempt to be God.

The glory of the gospel, however, is that while we destroy the world in our attempt to become God, God saves and redeems the world by becoming human. The cross of rebellion we erect to free ourselves from God and claim the world for ourselves, God uses to lay his final claim on us, and create a new world where we might work in peace and joy.

For now we can know who we really are, and who we were meant to be — obedient tenants in the vineyard of our loving Father God — who treats us not as tenants but as his sons and daughters.

*8*

# A Time for Celebration

### The Parable of the Wedding Feast
### Matthew 22:1-10
### Luke 14:15-24

Before entering a desert, the highways are posted with signs, "Last Chance," last chance for food and gas. Many interpreters have viewed the Parable of the Wedding Feast as a massive billboard standing in the Gospels with flashing lights and garish lettering spelling out a warning to all those who refuse the invitation of God into his Kingdom.

The parable is filled with fascinating details. The characters who refuse the invitation lend themselves to picturesque elaborations that can easily be identified with unchurched people we encounter every day. The drama of bums and riff-raff crowding into the magnificent banquet hall, snatching up the tasty morsels of elegantly prepared food, is irresistible to the imaginative mind. So preachers and interpreters have taken this simple story and have exaggerated it out of all proportion. They have allegorized it, moralized it, and theologically analyzed it to the point that there seems little left to say about it. Despite this over working, the parable still stands as a challenge. It is a good story, and the Bible preserves it for us to take our own shot at it.

## Two Accounts

The Parable of the Wedding Feast appears not only in Matthew but also in Luke. Luke's version is the shorter of the two, but he does elaborate on the refusals. Matthew makes of the story an elaborate allegory in which several parables are combined. The heavenly banquet has become a marriage feast of the king's son in Matthew, and the parable of the garments is added.

The excuses so prominent in Luke are not mentioned by Matthew. Matthew has some paying "no attention" to the invitation and others going so far as to murder the servants who bring the invitation. The anger of the host in Luke is expressed by the statement, "None of those men who were invited, I tell you all, will taste of my dinner." In Matthew this anger is intensified to the point that the king has his soldiers go out, burn down their city and kill all the people.

Most scholars preferring the shorter version of Luke consider it to be the original account, and Matthew's version, an allegorization of the parable to support his theme of conflict between Jesus and the Jewish leaders concerning the Messiahship of Jewish hope.

In our discussion of the parable we will consider both versions, but we will concentrate mainly on the Lukan version. The basic outline is the same in both accounts. A man gives a dinner and invites some particular guests. They refuse the invitation and suffer the consequences.

## The Kingdom

Luke places the parable in relation to a statement made to Jesus by a prominent and somewhat pompous Jew. He had just heard Jesus give the host a lesson in hospitality, that when he gives a feast he should invite the poor, the crippled, the lame, and the blind, and then he would be blessed. It was rather an awkward moment, and the man at the table was trying to save the situation with a pious platitude, "How happy are those who will sit at the table in the Kingdom of God." It was an insipid thing to say, and actually insulting to Jesus. For the man was sitting in the presence of Jesus who was the Messiah. But rather than acknowledging him and hailing his arrival as the coming of the Kingdom, the pompous old fool talked of the glory of a "Kingdom Day" far away in the future.

Now perhaps this was not intended as a direct insult. The man may not have heard the rumors that were going around about a young Nazarene claiming to be the Messiah, and that the Kingdom of God had come in him. But insult or ignorance, Jesus took this opportunity to stress once more that he was ushering in the future Kingdom and that those who refused to acknowledge him were saying "No" to God's invitation to come into the Kingdom. So he tells his parable about a king who gave a great banquet, sent out invitations, and the people refused to come.

In this parable, as in others we have dealt with, we must not identify the king with God. Particularly is this true with this parable, because if this is done, it creates impossible conclusions. For example, at the end of the story we see the poor, the crippled, the lame and the blind entering into the banquet hall. They are there, not because of the kindness of the king, but because of the sheer and unmitigated bitterness of the king toward the privileged guests who refused to come.

The host has suffered a deliberate insult. He is furious! He commands his servants to throw open the door to the riff-raff of the community. He may have felt that such an action would insult his original guests, showing them that the rabble of the streets were as good as they were and could easily take their places at his table. The kindest interpretation would be that the king didn't want the food to be wasted.

However, the conclusion cannot be avoided that the structure of the story presents the king's actions as motivated not by compassionate concern for the poor, but simply to spite the guests who refused to come. In the light of this understanding, to equate the king in the story with God is to do God a grave injustice. It is true that God, like the king, invites people into his feast, and the people refuse, but from this point on the similarity must be treated very cautiously.

The parable is not a picture of what God does, as much as it is an illustration of certain aspects of the Kingdom of God. Here, too, we must move very carefully, for this is not a total picture of the Kingdom, and many of the details do not apply. If all persons are to be welcomed into the Kingdom, it should be based on their own right by the promise of God. The inclusion of one person cannot depend on the rudeness of another. We are not saved by default. There can be nothing redemptive in an act of spite. The Kingdom of God was not opened to the Gentiles because the Jews refused. As Plummer[1] points out, "These were not asked simply because the others refused, and in order to fill the vacant places. They would have been asked in any case; but the others were asked first." God's plan is to move through the Jews to all the world with his invitation to participate in the Kingdom.

## Cultural Background

Kenneth Bailey,[2] of the Near Eastern School of Theology in Beirut, has pointed out that an interpreter must understand the cultural framework in which the parables were first told. He has gone directly to the peasants of the Middle East to discover the assumptions the teller of the parables must have had in mind about his listeners. In the discussion which follows, we are indebted to Dr. Bailey for his insights into the cultural situation that formed the background of this parable.

## "Was Giving"

The parable begins with a man who "was giving" a great feast. This implies not just one event but a series of events which made up one large event. The feast in Oriental culture is a very complex procedure. You do not simply set a date and then send out invitations. When a feast is first planned, the guests are sent an invitation to see if they will be able to come when a feast is made ready. After the responses are received to this first invitation, then the steers and the prize calves are butchered. You have to be assured of your guests before you kill the animals, for there is no way to preserve the unneeded food. Even a king possessed no freezer in his royal kitchen. When the first invitation goes out and a person accepts, he is under great moral obligation to attend, for he knows that his host has butchered the amount of meat necessary to feed all those who have accepted the primary invitation.

When the meat is cooked, the host sends his servants to the guests with his second invitation, which is more in the form of an announcement than an invitation. The servant's message is, "Come, for now all is ready."

### Excuses

Now follows the well-known list of excuses. Despite the fact that the shorter version of a parable is generally preferred, most scholars feel that Luke's addition directs attention to the real issue of the parable, namely the effort of the invited guests to avoid going to the supper.

The assumption of the parable is that the people who are giving the excuses have accepted the first invitation, but now that the definite time has come for them to attend, they have changed their minds.

The first man says, "I have bought land and must go see it." Now there is very little land for sale in the Middle East, and what there is, is mighty expensive. It is unthinkable that any man would risk the price he would have to pay for land by buying a field he had never seen. For one thing, water is very scarce and the buyer would have to see for himself just how the land was to be irrigated. To the Jews who first heard the parable this excuse was so ridiculous they undoubtedly laughed it down.

The second excuse is, "I have bought five pairs of oxen

and I am on my way to try them out." Now this, too, was unbelievable to the listeners. For in the days of our Lord, oxen were purchased in the market place. There was always a fenced-in area where the oxen could be tried, for a man would not think of buying a team of oxen until he had tried them out. The merchants even provided yokes that could be used by their customers to test the oxen. This man says "five pairs." This only heightens the dramatic impact of the excuse.

The third man says, "I have just married and therefore cannot come." In the Middle East women are simply not talked about in polite society. The relationship of a man and his wife is a very private affair. Even the faces of women are veiled to the world in many Oriental cultures. When he offers this excuse, he is not only presenting a weak reason for his refusal; he is being extremely crude, if not vulgar. It is interesting to note that the first two men extend their apologies with their excuses, but this man doesn't.

So the excuses offered are so unbelievable and unreal as to be humorous. They represent various ways in which three men insulted their host by offering flimsy reasons for not coming to his banquet.

### Postponement

Eta Linnemann[3] adds a somewhat different note to the general interpretation of the excuses. She points out that a banquet in the Middle East begins in the afternoon and goes on till after midnight, or even for several days. Therefore, the excuses offered may be seen not as deliberate refusals, but excuses for coming late. The men want to conduct their business and then come to the feast. However, when they finally arrive, they discover that there is no room left. Someone else has taken their place.

This would direct the spotlight of attention on the word "now" and the phrase, "My feast is ready now!" Many scholars agree with Linnemann that the decisive element of the parable is directed to the "nowness" of our reaction to the invitation. But we will deal with this later in the discussion.

## Room for More

The reaction of the host to these excuses was explosive. He was furious and sent his servants out into the streets and the alleys of the town to get guests to fill all the places at his table. In Luke's version there are two sendings — one into the city streets and the other out into the country lanes. Most scholars hold that the Early Church understood this second sending as a reference to going out to the Gentiles.

The important thing is that we are not to identify the refusers of the invitations with the whole Jewish nation. If you take the position that the three men of the parable represent the Jewish people who heard and refused the call of Jesus into the Kingdom, then you could only conclude that Jews are to be totally excluded from any opportunity for salvation. They had their chance and they refused it. Therefore the mission of the Church is to Gentiles only. You will find such an approach in many sermonic treatments of this parable. It is, however, difficult to justify, even when allegorizing this parable.

## "Will not Taste My Dinner"

This word "taste" is an interesting detail of the parable. In the Oriental culture the feast is first eaten by the honored guests; then the servants and the children partake. Some of the food is also given to the neighbors, and so on, until the food finally sifts out from a banquet to almost everybody in the village. Therefore, when Jesus has the host saying, "None of those men who are invited, I tell you all, will taste of my dinner," he is making the image as strong as he can. Even though many will taste the food even though they failed to attend the feast, these men who refused will not even get a taste of the food. This would seem to indicate complete exclusion from the Kingdom, even the side benefits of the Kingdom.

## Compel the People

This word "compel" also demands special attention. It has often been interpreted as justifying the forcing of people into the Kingdom by any means necessary. However, when seen in the culture patterns of Oriental people, such interpretations are not valid. Whenever a villager is invited to a feast, social protocol dictates, particularly in the case of some dignitary inviting an ordinary person, that you refuse. This is a way of complimenting your host. You are literally saying, "I am not worthy to come," not, "I don't want to come." Therefore, it is necessary to insist and repeat the invitation many times until the man is literally worn down and finally accepts. When Jesus uses the word "compel," he is only saying, "Do everything necessary to show the people you are sincere with the invitation, and you really want them to come."

I had a friend in college who was from Japan, and one day he said to me, "I have learned something very interesting here in America. When someone says to you that you should come over to their house sometime, this means you should not come. But when they say that you come over to their house Thursday evening about 7:30, that means come."

Now this is what the word "compel" implies. It means that the invitation is not a shallow or polite request. It is a very sincere desire to have the people come to the feast. The word "compel" literally means "convince them that you really mean it."

## Celebration

In this parable Jesus compares the Kingdom of God — as he frequently does — with a feast or banquet. This choice is not incidental, but the symbol shares in that which it symbolizes.

A feast is an extraordinary meal where the food is elaborate, plentiful and sumptuous. The atmosphere of a feast is festive, and it is a time for enjoyable fellowship. But most important, a feast, as Jesus uses it, is a commemoration — a celebration of an event. As the dictionary defines it, it is a time set apart for "sacred joy."

Eating is secondary to celebration, for the feast is an occasion with a purpose. An ordinary meal like breakfast, lunch, or dinner is intended primarily to satisfy our hunger. Not so with a feast. Its main purpose is to commemorate an event like a wedding or the visit of an important personage.

## Background

The Jews to whom Jesus was speaking were required by Mosaic Law to attend three major feasts: Passover, Feast of Weeks, or Harvest, and the Feast of Tabernacles, or Pentecost (Exodus 23:17, Deuteronomy 16:16). They were celebrations of great historic experiences of their nation. But first in their minds was the great Messianic Banquet, or Feast, which was to come in the future. For this they waited. For this they hoped. It would mark the day when God would break decisively into history and establish a new and glorious age. The enemies of the Jews would be destroyed, and Israel would be restored to its intended destiny. The symbol of this event was the Messianic Banquet. God would be the host, and it would be a feast of great joy.

Now it is against this background that Jesus tells his parable. When his listeners heard that some men refused to come to the feast, it would have meant to them a refusal to rejoice and celebrate the occasion of God's coming into history and a restored Israel.

So Christ meant it, for he had come, the great day had begun and few were aware of it. There was no rejoicing, no celebration. Instead, men denied him, or ignored him. He saw no joy in Israel over the coming of the Messiah. He saw only the stubborn refusal of people to accept his invitation into a new age.

So with us today. We refuse the invitation by our lack of joy. We stand outside the celebration and miss the opportunity which is ours. We refuse to rejoice because we think that the Kingdom has not yet come. We view the Kingdom, not as something being accomplished by God which we can now celebrate, but as something for which we as faithful people must roll up our sleeves, tighten our belts, and yet accomplish on this earth.

Pietism has marked faith with a frown — the frown of one seriously engaged in the gigantic task of bringing in the Kingdom of God. Fun and celebration are out of place because this is a time for work, the hard work of building the Kingdom.

The parable proclaims just the opposite. The Kingdom has come. God is accomplishing all things. Now is the time to celebrate and rejoice in what God is doing. The foolishness of the men who refused the invitations was their blindness to what was happening. They used the excuse that they had to work, when the time for work had passed and the hour of celebration was at hand. As God had labored six days and on the seventh day rested and celebrated, so now the great Sabbath celebration had dawned, and these men were refusing to stop their work and celebrate. In every sense they were breaking the holy "Sabbath of Celebration."

Auntie Mame rushes up the stairs shouting, "All the world's a banquet and most of us are starving to death." Now Auntie Mame was no Sunday-church-going Christian, but she shared the spirit of what Jesus was talking about in this parable. All the world is a banquet, because God has not forsaken his people but has come to them. The promise has been fulfilled. The new day has dawned and people are blind to it and refuse to celebrate. In so doing, people are insulting and denying God.

As their excuses reveal, they are too busy and concerned

with business — the buying and selling of cattle, the running of their homes. Now there is nothing wrong with accepting the responsibility of business and family. But when these stand in the way of our celebrating with God, then we are letting second best things shut out the best. We become so busy making a living that we fail to achieve a life — the new life that God's coming gives to us.

True, there is little good news in our world today. There is little to rejoice about in the realms of industry, economics, and politics. There are pollution, crime and corruption. But the mark of a Christian is one who undertakes to solve the problems of this world with a "happy heart." He has the Kingdom within himself and a joy that all the pessimistic headlines of the daily paper cannot overcome. If there is any hope that our monumental social problems are ever to be solved, it will be when people undertake them, not with a defeatist attitude, but as persons of "happy hearts" — those who have tasted victory and have seen a vision.

This parable says to us that if you have found no joy in faith, then you are refusing God's invitation to enter the Kingdom. For the Kingdom of God is God's presence and rule. Wherever people recognize God's presence and surrender to God's rule, there are people of "happy hearts," equal to any problem or task.

### Invites

The teaching of this parable is that we are invited into the Kingdom, not forced. The Jews had been required by law to attend their great religious feasts. But here Jesus implies that an invitation is extended by God as he opens his Kingdom feast. To make this parable a demand or an obligation, as is done so often in sermons, — i.e. that man **must** accept God's invitation, is to miss the whole thrust of the parable.

To accept under pressure, or to accept grudgingly because you think you have to, or should, can be no basis for true joy. Like the little boy who hates spinach. His mother says to him, "You'll eat it and you'll like it." Under his breath he says, "I'll eat it, but I won't like it." You cannot demand an emotion of a person. Joy is spontaneous and cannot be commanded.

## Unhappy People

An important underlying truth of the parable is not just what certain men did, or failed to do with God's invitation, but the type of persons these people were. They were "unhappy people." They saw no reason to celebrate, and that is why they refused to go to the feast. Their particular excuses are not really important. If a man sees no reason to rejoice, he can find all kinds of excuses and reasons for not attending God's feast.

There is an Arabian fable which tells about a man who went to his neighbor and asked to borrow a rope. "I can't lend it, because I am using it to tie up a pile of sand," his neighbor answered. "But," the man came back, "you can't tie up a pile of sand with a rope." To which his neighbor slyly replied, "Oh, yes you can. In fact you can do anything with a rope, when you do not wish to lend it to your neighbor."

So with the men in our parable. They did not want to celebrate or rejoice, and therefore they created ridiculous excuses for not attending.

## Free

When the gospel is proclaimed and we really hear that we are invited to the Kingdom, and this invitation is free, we should rejoice. The trouble is, most of us have been given demands, not invitations. We have been brainwashed with the high personal cost of redemption. We have been given invitations with a price tag. And the price is too high. It demands total and complete self-denial. It demands giving up all that is important in our lives. This we cannot afford, because we just don't have it within us to meet that high a cost.

A school teacher had saved her money for years to take the long-dreamed-of trip to Europe. She purchased her ticket on a great ocean liner. In her luggage she brought along a jar of peanut butter and a box of crackers in order to save money. Instead of eating the ship's food she sat alone in her cabin and munched on peanut butter sandwiches. When they were one day off the coast of France, her friend informed that when she purchased her ticket for the trip it had included all her meals. So there she was sitting in her room eating peanut butter when some of the most magnificent food she could ever have tasted went neglected.

So with us. So many of us are skimping through life munching peanut butter sandwiches when God has provided us with a free feast of joy. The good news of the gospel is enough reason for anyone to celebrate. The gospel is an invitation to dance, rejoice, enjoy a party. People need to hear the real gospel. They are refusing because someone has tried to sell them a high-priced ticket into heaven or a pass into paradise. What is needed is that the gospel be proclaimed for what it is — a free invitation by a loving father who has made all the preparations necessary. "Come," the gospel says, "for the feast is prepared and ready. All that is left to do is for you to enjoy it and rejoice in it."

### Now

An important word in the parable, as we have pointed out above, is the word "now." The problem of the Pharisees was not their refusal to believe in the good news of the Kingdom, but that they could not accept the fact that God's Kingdom was beginning now. They would not believe that in Jesus the Christ of the promise had come to usher in the new age. They simply saw no connection between Jesus' coming and God's presence.

This is true for many people today who call themselves

Christian. They accept Christ as a great example, and a sound moral teacher. They even acknowledge him as Savior — one who will save them from hell and enable them to get to heaven, but they do not really experience the presence of the living Lord — now!

Many Christians live in a continual Advent. They are always preparing but never performing — like an actor rehearsing lines in the dressing room after the curtain has gone up on the stage, or like a musician practicing at home for a concert that has already begun. So we study the Scripture but never apply it. We talk about God but never experience a living encounter with him.

Practice is important, but there is a time when we must stop practicing and start playing. Christ is saying in this parable, "It is the last half of the ninth inning. Bases are loaded. There are two outs. You are at the plate, bat in hand. The pitcher is winding up. The ball is pitched. The time is now. This is no time to say, 'Wait a minute, I need more practice.' This is the time to swing."

A young man once met a beautiful young French girl in college. He decided that before he approached her for a date he should totally prepare himself. So he enrolled in a course on French history and took a language class in French. At the end of the first semester he decided he was ready. But when he called her up on the phone, he learned that she had already become engaged to a football player who couldn't even speak good English.

Preparation is good except when the time calls for decisive action; then, to hesitate is certain disaster. It is like tabling an action in a committee meeting — just an indirect means of killing it. So with God's invitation — to postpone it is to kill it, for the time is now.

Now is the hour. Christ with this parable presents the Kingdom of God as a crisis hour. The Messianic Banquet is ready, and wise is the person who not only accepts, but accepts the invitation, NOW!

## Christ Accepts for Us

We have journeyed through this delightful parable, rich with insights into our relationship to the Kingdom of God. We have heard the invitation, and we have seen what happens when the invitation is refused. When we view the parable as a story, its structure would suggest that the impolite guests received exactly what they deserved. Their exclusion from the feast is not the fault of the host but the fickleness and the foolishness of the guests. The only conclusion seems to be that if we end up in heaven, we have no one to thank but God, our host. On the other hand, if we end up in hell we have no one to blame but ourselves. God has done everything short of forcing us into his Kingdom.

However, there is one more approach to the parable that should be mentioned. When we realize that we are on this side of the cross when we hear this story, we are in a far different position than those who first heard the story. We need to ask ourselves, what difference does the cross make? Did not Christ die on the cross because "man" was unable to accept the invitation? Did not Christ suffer precisely because "man" is stubborn and hard-hearted? What we failed to do, Christ our Savior accomplished for us.

Therefore, this parable stands not as a sign reading, "Last Chance," but as a sign of an invitation accepted for us. Christ on the cross accepts God's invitation for us, thereby placing us squarely in the center of the banquet hall at the table of God our King. We need to remember that we hear this parable of invitation as baptized Christians. We are not outside looking in. We are at the banquet. As Luther points out, by our baptism we are literally lifted up out of the realm of damnation and placed securely into the realm of salvation.

Now this does not mean that the issue is closed. We still are responsible people before God. Despite the fact that Christ has accepted for us, we yet need to accept our acceptance. We need to surrender to what our Lord has done for us and enjoy and celebrate our presence at God's great feast. But we are in a different position than the men of our parable. We are not given an invitation to come to the feast, but to enjoy the feast to which we have been brought.

We can accept and attend a dinner and refuse to eat. We can refuse to enter into the festivities. This is where the freedom of our wills enters in. We can, if we choose, starve to death at a table of plenty. Or we can, as God so constantly hopes we will do, relax, rejoice, surrender to his gracious generosity and enjoy all that he has so abundantly provided for us.

In Christ the Kingdom of God is ours. We are not awaiting an invitation, or even considering whether to accept or not; we are in the midst of it. Now it only remains for us to become what we are, because of what Christ has done for us. We are honored and happy guests at the table of our God.

### The Parable of the Wedding Garments

Now Matthew adds a parable to the Parable of the Wedding Feast, a story about a man who is thrown out of the banquet hall because he did not have on appropriate clothes. It is important that we briefly consider it, for it is directed to those who are at the feast, and we ended our discussion of the Parable of the Wedding Feast exactly on that note. As baptized Christians, we find ourselves not faced with what we are going to do with the invitation, but what we are going to do once we are there.

### Victim or Villain

When one looks at the story of the parable in and of itself, the way in which the man got into the feast is an important consideration. The implication is that he was suddenly confronted with the invitation and was not quite sure of where he was going.

You recall the king was frustrated and furious at the refusals of his guests and sent his servants out into the streets to gather up all they could find and compel them to come to the party. Our poor embarrassed friend was one of those hurried into the banquet hall. Suddenly he is singled out by the king and condemned for his lack of wedding garments. Not only this, but he is thrown bodily back out into the streets.

As the story stands, this poor fellow seems to be the victim of the story rather than the villain. When he got up in the morning, he had no idea that before the day was over he was going to be in the king's house sitting down to dinner as an honored guest. Even if he had suitable clothes to wear at such a fancy function, he had no chance to go home and put them on. The treatment he receives at the hand of the king seems most unfair.

However, when we study the social protocol of the days of our Lord we discover that it was the custom of a host to provide adequate garments for his guests to wear at the feast. This throws an entirely new light on the parable. Now we see a man who receives a rare and unusual opportunity to be included as a guest at the banquet hall of the king, but who refuses to change his clothes and put on the appropriate dress that was provided by his host. That makes a great deal of difference. Instead of a man victimized by the fact that his clothes are not good enough for the party, we see a man stubbornly refusing to change in order to fit a new and festive occasion.

The lesson which our Lord intends to teach with this little story gradually emerges. He is saying that the Kingdom of God is a gift freely given to all, but getting into the Kingdom is only the beginning. The decisive issue for those who are in the Kingdom is their willingness to accept the change that is also given by God. Call it growth in grace, maturing of faith, sanctification — give it any name you desire; it all comes down to the fact that once we are at the feast of the king, we must not resist the change that he desires to bring about in us.

Jesus is here pointing out that life in the Kingdom is dynamic. It is an experience of being changed by your host.

Too often we think of life in the Kingdom, or salvation, as a goal achieved by good works or as a gift received by grace, but in either case once you are in you're in and that's it.

In the past, the church has been pictured as a ship floating in a sea of sinking sinners. The lifeline is thrown out and the drowning sinners are pulled into the safety and security of the ship of salvation. When all are aboard, all is well. We are baptized as babies, or we make a decision as adults. We dash down the sawdust trail in one denomination, or we graduate from catechism in another. And we're in. That's it.

The Parable of the Wedding Garments calls this "membership" concept of salvation into serious question. It says getting in isn't enough. It is only the beginning. The real issue is staying in, and to do that, you need to be willing to have God work a change in you.

The book of Acts, and especially Paul in his epistles, describes the Christian not as one who has been saved, but as one who is in the process of being saved. Salvation is not a **product** we possess but a **process** in which we participate. Faith is an on-going experience. The Kingdom is open-ended. Salvation is a dynamic process of growth.

We have all known the professor who, twenty-five years ago, wrote out his lectures and still mumbles through the dog-eared pages of his notes. Such a professor was once passed up for an appointment as head of the department. He went to the dean and protested. "After all," he said, "do not my twenty-five years of teaching experience count for something?" To which the dean answered, "My dear friend, you have not had twenty-five years of teaching experience. You have had only one year of teaching experience repeated twenty-five times."

Now it is not easy to face the fact that this also applies to our experience of faith within the realm of salvation. The length of our participation within the Kingdom of God might be only a static experience, repeated over and over again, with no change or growth. Who hasn't known the individual who had a religious experience at his entrance into the

Kingdom and has attempted to exist on the momentum of that one experience his whole life through? He retells it over and over again, but he never moves beyond it.

For many of us, this is a difficult word to hear. We cling to the comforting idea that Christ never changes. We live in a world that is constantly changing, and changing so fast that we can't seem to keep up with it. We know what Alice in Wonderland meant when she said, "We have to run as fast as we can just to stay where we are." This isn't easy. That is why the intellectuals of our day refer to this constant demand for rapid change as "Future Shock."

It would be wonderful if we could retreat to the church where nothing changes and always remains the same. Or would it? For such a church would be little different than a graveyard. For life is change, and as difficult as change is, it is a vital aspect of what it means to be alive.

Like the man who just turned sixty-five. He was asked by his younger friend how it felt becoming a senior citizen. The elderly man replied, "It feels great, when I consider the alternative." And this is true; the only alternative to change is death.

Bonhoeffer, the great Christian martyr of our century, challenges the church to a growing faith in one of his last books, *No Rusty Swords.*[4] The point he makes is that the sword of faith must have a cutting edge and that means an edge constantly sharpened and polished anew.

The Parable of the Wedding Garments says to us that we must have a faith that is constantly fitted to new garments — garments that are freshly and creatively fashioned and designed to meet the changing needs of each new day. It is true that Christ never changes, but this parable is about the change that he desires to work constantly in us. And he never changes in his desire to change us.

Wouldn't it be interesting if next Sunday morning the worship service we attended would be a "Come As You Are Service?" That is, everyone who attended worship would come dressed in garments that would reflect just where he or she stood in the process of salvation and life in the Kingdom. Some would be dressed in their baptismal gowns, for their faith never got off the ground. They were brought to the font by their parents and they have been brought to the church ever since. Quite a few would be dressed in the clothes they wore to Sunday school twenty years ago, because their faith has never moved beyond the basic Bible-story stage. Most people would be wearing their confirmation robes, for catechism was the point at which they stopped learning about faith.

Many, if they were perfectly honest, would have to borrow clothes from their grandparents, because they never possessed any real faith of their own. Their attitude is, "If it's good enough for Grandpa, it's good enough for me." They are satisfied with the "old time religion" which isn't very old at all. It just seems that way.

And there would be some attending church with nothing on at all because the little faith that they might have once had has dried up and has been easily dusted away by the passing of the years.

It would be a strange sight indeed — more like a costume party than a group of contemporary Christians worshiping their Lord. But strange and shocking as this experience might be, at least we would have little trouble recognizing the validity and the value of the Parable of the Wedding Garments. Without a doubt the words of our Lord would take on dynamic meaning as he spoke to us through the words of the king in the parable, "Friend, what are you doing (in this day and age, in my church) dressed like that?"

We dare not leave the parable here. For our Lord tells this parable not to condemn us and throw us out into the streets. Rather, he tells this parable to help us and enable us to realize that change is an inevitable consequence of being in the Kingdom. He is going to work a change in us, and through us, constant changes within his church.

But one more word needs to be added. This does not mean that all change in the church is good. In the parable the new garments are provided by the king. So in the Kingdom and within the church. God works the change. Therefore we must remain critical and evaluate every challenge to change. Test change to see if it is of God. If it is not of God, defy it. If it is of God, dare it.

Change is not easy. It demands that we live close to God's Word so that we remain sensitive to his will. We need to carefully evaluate every new thing. Where the change is wrong, it must be resisted — never resisted simply because it is new or different, but because it is not of God. In the Kingdom of God we are called to be flexible but alert, sensitive but sensible, responsive but responsible, critical but courageous. Test change. If it is not of God, defy it. If it is of God, dare it.

## 9

# The Third Coming

### The Parable of the Wise and Foolish Virgins
### Matthew 25:1-13

This is the story of five girls who missed out on a party. It begins with ten girls who went out to meet a bridegroom, and attend with him a wedding feast. The groom was delayed, and when he finally arrived the lamps of the foolish girls were going out. While they ran to the store to get more oil, the bridegroom entered the feast and the doors were closed. So the foolish girls missed out on a party.

Exegetes are quick to point out that the details of the parable do not agree with what is generally known about the wedding customs of the time. One wonders where the bride was while all this was going on. Is the groom on the way to the bride's home to hold the wedding there? This was not generally the custom. And the lamps — Harvey[1] finds difficulty here. The small domestic lamps that are suggested would easily be blown out. Storm-lamps made of horn gave very subdued light and would not be very festive for a wedding. Torches were frequently used for night processions, but they were made of cones of wood coated with pitch and would require no oil. The only conclusion would seem to be that the author of the story is not appealing to a familiar image of a wedding to illustrate an aspect of the Kingdom. Rather he is creating a story that might have happened even though it was not according to well-established custom. This, together with the fact that the symbolic number ten is used and the wise and foolish virgins are divided equally, leads many scholars to conclude that the parable was a creation of the Early Church to deal with the delayed coming of Jesus. Julicher, Dodd and Jeremias on the other hand, regard it as an authentic parable of Jesus. Then there are interpreters such as Bultmann and Klostermann who see the parable as a creation of the Early Church, but based on an original version of a story told by Jesus during his ministry.

### Preparedness

Most of the interpretations revolve about the idea of preparedness. A. M. Hunter states that it is a parable about "ten village girls on their way to a wedding, five of whom skimped their preparations and lived to rue their carelessness."[2] Hunter placed this among the crisis parables spoken by Jesus, warning his hearers that the Kingdom of God is moving toward them. They are headed for certain disaster if, like the foolish girls, they are caught unprepared.

Preparedness is the mark of those who live wisely "in between the times." This is exactly where we find ourselves today — in between the first coming of Christ in the flesh and his final coming in glory. Since we do not know when that final day will be, we must live in a constant state of preparedness. Like a hunter waits with his gun raised and his finger on the trigger ready to take exact aim and fire when the resting birds take flight, so we wait, ready for the decisive moment of action. Professor Moule puts it in colorful terms when he points out that "the kick-off has already taken place," and our job is to be ready at all times "to receive the next pass."[3]

## Delay

Eta Linnemann[4] adds the word "delay" to the idea of preparedness. She says that the parable was created by the Early Church to teach that true readiness takes into consideration the fact that Christ might be delayed.

This says something very important to us concerning the true nature of faith. Faith should not be shattered by changes. Faith should be flexible and ready to cope with whatever arises. As in the realm of nature so in the realm of faith, survival is dependent on one's ability to adapt to changing conditions.

How often people say that they simply can't worship in church if the liturgy changes, or the pastor resigns, or the building is remodeled, or the communion practices are revised. A faith that cannot adjust to these minor experiences of change is certainly unprepared to wait for an unpredictable Lord. It is the false faith of the foolish maidens that was not flexible enough to endure the surprised delay of the bridegroom.

## Suddenness

Jeremias[5] stresses not only the idea of preparedness and delay, but he adds that when God comes it will be sudden and unexpected.

The mistake here is to conclude that God is hiding behind a bush ready to pounce on us when we least expect it. All of us have played this game with children. We come behind them, grab hold of them and then are delighted when they jump with shocked surprise. God is not like that. God is not hiding behind a door ready to jump out and surprise us at an unexpected moment to see what our reactions will be. Nor is God the suspicious lover who checks up on his loved one by showing up unexpectedly hoping to catch him in a compromising position. This is not the reason for God withholding the time and manner of his coming. He withholds this information because it is not necessary that we know. God assumes that people of faith should be ready to receive him whenever he comes. The Christian style of life should not be like special manners we assume when company comes. Nor is it like Sunday clothes we dress up in for special occasions. We should be like the person who is such a good housekeeper that we are always ready for company to drop in. God doesn't phone ahead and tell us when he is coming because he assumes it should not be necessary. We should be living in such a way that at any moment we are ready to receive him.

To understand this suggestion of the parable we really have to redefine our idea of preparedness. For most of us, preparation implies something different we have to do for a special occasion. In the New Testament concept of preparedness, it is a way of life. The idea that preparedness is something special would only create an unbearable tension, particularly when the special occasion is constantly postponed.

Every so often a group of people will read the signs of the time and decide that Jesus is on his way. They will sell everything they own, dress in white robes and go to the highest hill around to wait for him. This implies that the affairs of ordinary life are not really a suitable state of preparedness. We have to do something special. However, in the parable, the girls with their lamps were engaged in an ordinary function of life. The point of the parable is that five of the girls were unprepared because what they were doing was substandard. They were not doing anything wrong. They were doing exactly what the five wise girls were doing. An additional supply of oil was not something extra but something any person should possess when going out to meet a bridegroom at night.

A spare tire in the trunk is the normal equipment of an automobile. It is not an extra. It is not something we put in the trunk only when we are going to take a long trip. We keep it in the trunk even when our car is parked in the garage. Only a fool would think of driving a car without a spare tire. So the point of the parable is not readiness at all times to put your house in order, but living in an orderly house at all times so that the coming of the guests requires no extra activity. The optimist says, "Live today as if this day were the first day of your life." The pessimist says, "Live today as if it might be the last day of your life." The Parable of the Wise and Foolish Virgins says, "Live right today, and it doesn't matter whether it is the first or the last day of your life."

## Wisdom

Our parable also speaks about wisdom. Now this is not a particularly popular word today. We tend to use the term "wise" in the derogatory sense, such as "a wise guy." And this is nothing new or typical only of our own age. On the facade of the Cathedral of Strasbourg, the ten virgins have been sculptured in a fashion that is artificially beautiful, but not very biblical. For here the five wise virgins are depicted as smug and complacent. It is as if they were saying, "I told you so." This does not represent the attitude of the wise virgins in our parable. The word that is translated "wise" actually means "to keep the eyes open," or, as Eta Linnemann suggests, "sharp." Five of the girls in our parable were wise because they were going about an ordinary activity of a wedding ceremony with their "eyes open." They were equipped to deal with an emergency or change in plans that might arise. And that's not being smug. That's being "sharp" in any age.

## Role Playing

Wallace[7] takes a rather unusual approach to this parable and sees in it a warning against hypocrisy, sham and religious imitation. The foolish virgins were just role playing. They looked and acted like the responsible wise maidens, but when the decisive hour came, they were unable to keep up their false appearances.

Wallace believes that God brings testing experiences upon his church for the purpose of separating the genuine from the imitators. This parable is a warning that we should not play games with God.

## The Final Judgment

The theme of warning is further developed by Dan Via in his interpretation of the parable. He believes that this is a parable not of what **will** happen, but what **might** happen. The parable "suggests that one of the possibilities of human existence may be lost. When a crisis is not responsibly met, the opportunity for further action may be cut off."[8] The parable is therefore directed against those who take salvation lightly. True, salvation is a free gift of grace, but we who receive it must not assume a smug attitude toward free grace and take the position that the world and God owe us a living.

The foolish virgins superficially supposed that they would be taken care of somehow. "If we run out of oil, our friends will help us, or the merchant will still be up, or even if we are late the groom will not lock us out."[9] But the foolish girls miscalculated the situation and the parable ends with the finality of a slamming door, shut, locked and barred.

This suggests that we should never be smug or complacent about our own salvation. It is a personal promise proclaimed in the gospel. But salvation must never become an unconditional guarantee that we hold over the head of God as a demand. Many interpreters see this parable as presenting the possibility that salvation may be lost.

Karl Barth has referred to damnation as the "impossible possibility."[10] It is impossible because Christ has destroyed sin, death, and the Devil, and by this daring deed freely given us the new life. But damnation is possible because we must constantly keep in mind the background against which our salvation is a reality. Hell and damnation are a real possibility, for they are absolutely necessary for us to appreciate what Christ has done for us. If the existence of hell and the possibility of damnation are unreal, then our Lord's sacrifice and death are but meaningless gestures and the cross is a sham.

When our Lord speaks of damnation as the final closing of the door — as some believe he does in this parable — he is not intending primarily to frighten us, or to hold the threat of punishment over our heads. Rather, he is disclosing the reality of damnation that we might more fully appreciate what he has done for us. When we hear the statement that hell is real, we should not fear it as a threat but rejoice in the promise of our redemption. Hell is presented as a real possibility of judgment not to reveal what will happen to some of us but what could have happened, and should have happened, to all of us. For none of us, even the best of us, deserves anything other than the fiery destruction of hell.

We who are in Christ are like people rescued from a burning ship. Having been rescued by our Savior, we stand on the shore watching the burning inferno. It is no illusion. It is a reality. We can see the light from the fire and feel the heat from the flames. As we stand there, safe on the shore, we keep saying to ourselves, "There, but for Christ, would have been my fate." So Christ tells his parables of final judgment and the torment of those who are judged and found wanting, that we might never lose sight of the burning ship or the fact that this should have been our fate, if it had not been for him and his cross. As we stand in and with Christ, the burning ship is our great impossible possibility.

## Salvation Is a Joy

This parable also suggests that salvation is a state of joy. As we have pointed out above, the attitude of the foolish maidens is an important issue in the parable. They were not taking their responsibilities seriously enough. And because of this they failed to get everything out of the situation in which they found themselves. The parable is not intended to be a literal description of what is literally and finally true of the Last Judgment. Rather, it is the lesson that our attitude toward the salvation we receive as a free gift of grace determines how much we get out of the fact that we are a redeemed and a saved people. The issue here is not that some are saved and others are damned. But it is the profound observation that when we fail to fully appreciate our redemption, then redemption becomes meaningless, and we actually close the door on an experience of joy that salvation should bring to us.

The tragedy of the parable is not that the closed door robbed these maidens of their lives, it simply robbed them of the joy of the feast. The parable does not end with servants rushing forth from the house with swords to bring revengeful punishment on the foolish maidens. No, it simply ends on the decisive fact that these girls missed out on the party. The foolish maidens engaged in the task of waiting for the bridegroom. They brought the needed lamps, and they woke up in time to greet the bridegroom, but the point is their preparation was limited. They did something, but they didn't do enough to be included in the party.

So this parable speaks to us saying, "Not only prepare but prepare completely." Go all the way. Like the little boy who discovered when he tried to jump over the mud puddle, "Half way is not enough."

## Tinkering with Trivials

Preparedness, delay, and suddenness are main issues of the parable, but when we look at the parable as a story there is another lesson that comes through. The foolishness of the girls was not just their lack of preparation, or their failure to anticipate the delay, or the sudden coming of the bridegroom, but the fact that when the bridegroom finally came, they were more concerned with their lamps than with the bridegroom.

True, they were fools because they were unprepared, but

they also made fools of themselves over their lack of preparedness. They knew that the bridegroom had come. His arrival was loudly announced. It was literally shouted up and down the streets. And interestingly enough, there is no indication in the parable that they could not have participated in the procession without light in their lamps. But rather than forgetting about their lamps and taking the chance that in the excitement of the groom's coming they might just get into the feast without lighted lamps, they turned their backs on the bridegroom and ran in the other direction. Undoubtedly they wanted to make a good impression on this special occasion. After all, it isn't every day that one's friend gets married. But their concern for themselves in the presence of the bridegroom is what labels them for all time as fools.

If Jesus did originally tell this parable, perhaps in the back of his mind was the experience he encountered again and again among his people. He came as a bridegroom offering them the great celebration of redemption, and they were so busy tinkering with their lamps that they failed to hear or even see him. The Pharisees spent their whole lives concerned for God and his truth, yet when Jesus, the incarnate Son of God, stood in their midst and spoke to them, they failed to see him for who he really was. They tinkered with their lamps of the Law and overlooked the bridegroom. Is it any wonder that Jesus wept over Jerusalem? So many foolish virgins. So many closed doors. Jerusalem was a city of people tinkering with their lamps. What good is it to watch and wait, when, fools that we are, we ignore the Lord when he comes?

I remember visiting the Vatican and standing with a group of tourists who were being shown the priceless art treasures and great masterpieces of this holy city. The guide paused in his lectures and asked if there were any questions. One little lady from the States immediately spoke up, "Where can we buy some souvenirs?" Standing in the midst of priceless beauty, her only concern was where she could buy cheap junk. What could be more foolish than to stand in the presence of greatness and tinker with the trivial? Yet this is what our Lord experienced. He came as the bridegroom to the marriage feast, and people ignored him and tinkered with their lamps. He came as the light of the world to give us eternal light so that we would never have to dwell in darkness again. And where were we — running off to the store to buy oil for our own failing lamps so that we might make a good impression before God. Fools. Certainly the title fits us all, for what could be more foolish than to stand in the presence of greatness and tinker with trivials?

### The Third Coming

One last interpretation needs to be considered. This is to approach the parable as pure story. When we eliminate all the details which tend to suggest allegorization, then we are able to see the pure plot of the story. For example, when the terms "wise" and "foolish," "virgins" and "bridegroom," "oil" and "lamps," are eliminated, that which is left is the basic structure of the story. It consists of two events, a procession and a feast. The plot formed by these two events is simple. If a person does not participate in one, he cannot take part in the other. Fail to be a part of the procession, and you will be shut out from the feast. Or it might be stated, what we do today determines what we will be able to do tomorrow.

If the parable which Jesus originally told has been overlaid with details to serve allegorical ends, then the reduction of the story to its basic plot might suggest something of the original story Jesus told. Christ was confronted with the firm Jewish belief in the great Messianic Banquet of the future. Again and again he attempted to point out that the Jews were failing to see what was happening now because their minds were so firmly absorbed with the future feast of God.

The foolish virgins in the parable did not take part in the bridegroom's procession. The reason they did not — namely, their lack of oil — was not as important as the simple fact that they did not participate in the procession. Efforts to

134

discover what the lack of oil signifies can easily divert the attention of the listener away from the basic issue of non-participation. Even the concern with the delay and then the sudden coming of the bridegroom can mislead the listener away from the decisive moment of the story when the door is shut. The question of first importance is not why did the girls fail to participate in the procession, but why was the door shut? And the answer the story gives is that they did not participate in the procession. To the Jews who first heard this story it could only mean that their treatment of the bridegroom's arrival was the decisive issue of the story. They did not participate in his procession. They did not follow him. And if they did not follow him, they could not possibly go into the wedding feast.

Now what does this parable say to us today, to those who might wonder if they are to have a part in the world which is to come? The parable story answers that we can be as certain of heaven as we are certain of this moment. If we stand in a right relationship with God now in Christ, we will be in a right relationship to God then.

Our questions concerning the Last Judgment are also answered by the thrust of the story. The Scripture really says very little about the details of this experience. This at first seems strange that something so vital to our eternal destiny should be so slighted in the total revelation of Scripture. But in the light of this parable such limited descriptions of the Last Judgment are understandable because the decisive issue of our eternal destiny is not what happens then but what is happening now. As we surrender to Christ now, and trust in him now, as we participate in and with him now, our future is assured. We do not have to wonder and wait until the final judgment day. We are being judged now. We are not in the position of the virgins waiting for the bridegroom to come. For those who are in Christ, the bridegroom has already come, not in glory but in the presence of the Holy Spirit. And he has taken us unto himself.

There are three comings of Christ — one in the flesh, one

in glory, and the third, his continual coming through the Holy Spirit by way of the Word and the sacraments. In salvation history, the first and the second coming are the decisive events. But for us personally as believers, the third coming is the most decisive. We cannot go back to the cross on Calvary, nor can we suddenly jump ahead to that day when he shall come in triumph. Our moment is now as we stand before the living Lord. The Parable of the Wise and Foolish Virgins speaks a different word to us than when it was first told. Today the plot of the parable — "participation in the procession means attending the feast" — assures us that as we stand in a right relationship with our Lord now, we are rightly related to the past event of his coming in the flesh, and the future event of his coming in glory. As we are taking part in the procession now, we can be assured that we shall participate in all that is yet to come.

The decisive issue is not wisdom or foolishness, filled or empty lamps, but being in the procession so that future doors will not be closed to us.

Therefore we rejoice that we are in the procession of the bridegroom that has come. We do not worry about the past, nor fret about the future. We need no lamps to light his way, for Christ our Lord is the light of the world and lights our way, and most important of all, he opens all doors for us.

## *10*

# The Tragedy of the One Talent Man

### The Parable of the Talents
### Matthew 25:14-30
### Luke 19:12-27

Alongside the great tragedies of literature such as *Hamlet*, we should place the story of this parable, for it is the tragedy of the one talent man. The parable tells of three men and what happened to them. The first two men are only the background against which the tragedy of the one-talent man is played.

### Two Versions

There are two versions of this parable, one in Luke, the other in Matthew. The account in Luke at first is hardly recognizable as a parable. The man who goes away on a trip in Matthew becomes a nobleman who goes away to be made king in Luke. The three servants of Matthew become ten servants in Luke. But the greatest difference is the notation in Luke that the master was a hated man, which seems to have nothing to do with the faithful servants and their wise use of the money entrusted to them. At the end of the Lukan version the hated nobleman, returning as king, rewards his faithful servants, takes the money away from the unfaithful servant, and gives it to the servant who earned ten coins. Then the king commands, "Now, as for these enemies of mine who did not want me to be their king: bring them here and kill them." Apparently this did not include the unfaithful servant, so he gets off much better than in the version according to Matthew. In Luke, all that happens to him is that his money is taken from him and given to another, but in Matthew, he is thrown "outside in the darkness; and there he will cry and gnash his teeth."

Most scholars believe Luke reconstructs the parable into an allegory of Jesus' ascension. Because of this elaborate reconstruction by Luke, the Matthew version is much more fruitful for its preaching values.

## The Facts of the Case

Therefore let us look at some of the basic facts of Matthew's account of the story. A man is about to leave on a trip, and he calls his servants to him to assign their responsibilities. He does this by giving to each servant a certain portion of the property for them to manage. Now this confronts us with the first important word, "gave."

## He Gave to Them

The master gave to each according to his ability. Now giving is not only a key word in this parable, but it is a key word to the totality of Scripture. God is a giving God. His "givingness" is called grace. In the beginning, God gives his newly created world to man and calls him to be a good steward over it. God gives the covenant to his people to assure them of their relationship to him. God gives deliverance to the Israelites when they are enslaved in Egypt. God gives the Law and the prophets, and finally he gives his son to redeem the world.

Many believe that the important religious question is,

"What must I do to get?" The question of grace is, "What must I do with what I have been given?" So with the men in our parable; they are not confronted with a job that they have to do in order to get something, but they are given a gift which they must manage and use.

## Not Equal

In the parable, the gifts were given by the master, taking into consideration the abilities of each servant. All persons are not created equal. And God knows this and never requires of us more than we can do. But he does require that we do the best we can with what we have. However, envy enters in. We recognize the outstanding talents of others. Our ambition outruns our abilities, and because we cannot do as much as we would like to do, we will not do as much as we can. So with the man in our parable; he was obviously not equal to his fellow servants. So the master gave him only one thousand dollars as compared to five thousand and two thousand that were given to the other two servants. He was given less, not because the master disliked him, but because the master wanted to be fair. The reason for the servant's reaction is difficult to establish. It may have been the result of envy, or jealousy, or he might just have been bitter and took the attitude, "I would have done more, if only I had been given more."

Edward Everett Hale once said, "I am only one, but I am one. I cannot do everything, but I can do something. I will not let what I cannot do interfere with what I can do." This was perhaps the attitude that the master desired to discover in his backward servant. But he did not.

## Faithfulness

When the master returned, he called the servants in for an accounting of what had occurred while he was gone. The servant who had received five thousand dollars came in and handed over ten thousand dollars. The servant who had been given two thousand dollars came in and presented to the master four thousand dollars. It is important to note that the servant who gained five thousand dollars for the master did not receive more honor or reward than the one who had gained only two thousand. To both men the master said exactly the same words, "Well done, good and faithful servant. You have been faithful in managing small amounts, so I will put you in charge of large amounts." This would mean that with the master all faithfulness ranks the same. For he who does his best does all. So with God, faithfulness is not evaluated by degrees. You are either faithful or you are not. It is like being pregnant. You cannot be a little pregnant. So you cannot be a little faithful. Now it is true that the parable says that he who is faithful in little things will be faithful in great. But it says nothing about little or great faithfulness. You are either faithful or you are not.

These men were commended not for their success but for their faithfulness, which means that faithfulness is not the same as faultlessness. We might try and fail, but we are still faithful for having tried. Martin Luther King, when asked what he wanted on his tombstone, remarked, "He tried to love somebody." Note the profound insight here of true faithfulness — not that he did love, but that he **tried** to love. And not everybody but somebody. This is faithfulness: trusting in God, we undertake the task presented to us and do the best we can. Though we might fail, we are still faithful.

### The Owner Benefits

An important point of the parable is that the servants work and wisely use their talents not for themselves but that the possessions of the master might be increased. So often, when we are called to work in the Kingdom, we enter into the work with selfish motives. God will be pleased with our efforts and will surely bless us in a special way. The truth is, we are called to work in the Kingdom that others might receive what we have already been given. We witness and work, not to achieve more blessing for ourselves, but in order to be given more responsibility and greater tasks to do.

In the parable, the rewards the faithful servants received were not a bonus, or a raise in salary, or even a paid vacation, but greater responsibility. "You have been faithful in managing small amounts, so I will put you in charge of larger amounts."

## What We Fail to Use We Lose

This is the warning that runs throughout the parable — what we fail to use we lose. Cox,[1] in the *Torch Commentaries*, states that this parable was originally a warning to the Jewish nation, or at least to their leaders, that they were not to preserve unused their priceless spiritual heritage. Rather, they were to risk even possible corruption of their heritage in a great adventure of extending the Word of God out beyond the limitations of their own nation to the Gentiles. If they did not take this risk, they would lose what they had.

So for us. A church is placed on a corner in a particular community, not to preserve the Christian heritage and defend it against all aggressors, but to invest itself in the life of that community — if need be, to die for that community. When God calls a congregation to account for its existence, he does not want to hear that we have held our own, kept up the mortgage payments on the building, protected the liturgy from corruption, and the Bible from misinterpretation, so that we can now hand back to him all that he has given us in the same mint-like condition, as it was when we first received it. No, God wants to know that we have used the Gospel by giving it away with our services.

One of my students told that when he was a little boy he won a cake at a church social. It was the first thing that he had ever won, and he was so proud of it that he wouldn't let anyone even touch it. He took it home and put it on a table in his room and just looked at it. He couldn't bring himself to eat or share with his family that prized possession. Then one day he noticed that the cake was starting to discolor with stale mold. It was good for nothing but to be thrown away. A cake is meant to be eaten, and unless we use it, we lose it.

To use is to increase. To neglect is to lose. You don't have to burn up books and tear down libraries to destroy knowledge; you just have to refuse to read. You don't have to insult a person to lose his friendship; just forget about him. Fail to call him or write a letter to him and before you know it he will be gone. So this parable extends its point into every area of our life. What we fail to use, we lose.

This parable points up an energy crisis — a radically different energy crisis than now faces our nation — for this is a crisis not of exhausted energy but of unused energy. We run out of natural gas because we use too much of it; but just the opposite is true concerning the energy of grace. We run out of grace when we don't use it. The more we use grace, the more we receive of it.

### Lazy or Afraid

The master in the parable condemns the servant by calling him "a bad and lazy servant." However, the man says of himself that he was afraid. These different attitudes toward the man's failure are extremely suggestive. What appeared to the master as laziness was, if we can accept the servant's self-analysis, fear. These are two quite different personal qualities.

Granskou focuses in on the word of the servant that he was afraid and sees in the parable a comparison between the importance of risk in the life of business and the importance of risk in religious life. He points out that religious establishments are often too cautious. He adds that all people "ought to be as daring in religion as they are in business."[2]

## A Tragedy in Three Acts

So far we have looked at some traditional approaches to this parable. Now let us approach it from a different angle and see if we can discover why the man himself, as well as his story, was a tragedy.

### Act One

This is the story of a man who thought that he was doing right, when he was actually doing wrong. Now it is tragic when someone knowingly does something wrong, like robbing a store or stealing a car. He may have good reasons for doing it. He may have all kinds of rationalizations to explain why he did it, but he knows what he did was wrong and he admits it.

Not so with our tragic hero. He thought he was doing the right thing. No one forced him to do what he did. There were no circumstances that tempted him to do an evil thing. In the freedom of his own conscience, he made a decision which he thought was right. He knew that the master was a hard man. He also knew that his own abilities were limited. So he thought the matter through and listened to his own conscience which said to him, "This money doesn't belong to you so you had better not take any chances with it. Better to be safe than sorry." So he took the money, dug a hole, and buried it in the ground.

Now this should be first a warning to us all that the conscience is not always a good guide. For the most part, the conscience is generally conservative. It operates rather well as a braking system when temptation attempts to push us into a reckless action, but it is not always a good steering mechanism. When we are lost and don't know which way to go, the conscience is helpless. What we need is help from outside ourselves. The conscience is too much a part of us to give us much aid.

It is important to note here that the man in our parable,

knowing his own lack of ability, could have sought help. He could have given the money to an expert to invest for him, or he could have put it in the bank. But he would not face and accept his limitations.

So our tragic hero went his way and did his own thing, thinking all the while that he was doing right. And no one is so wrong as the person who doesn't know that he is wrong. For him there is no hope. Common sense teaches that the Lord helps those that help themselves. But the gospel teaches that the Lord, in many cases, cannot help those who are stubbornly determined to help themselves.

## Act Two

When the one talent man is finally forced to face an accounting of his stewardship, and it is pointed out to him how wrong his actions have been, he takes the position that it wasn't his fault. He tries to place the blame on someone else. He says he did what he did because his master was a hard man.

It is difficult to help a man who is wrong and doesn't know it. It is twice as difficult to help a man who is wrong and won't admit it. And our tragic hero is both. If the man had admitted his guilt and thrown himself on the mercy of the master, our story might have had a completely different ending. This is particularly true in our relationship to God. We are lost, not because we are guilty of doing wrong, but because of our unwillingness to face our guilt and admit it. God stands ready and willing to help those who seek after and request his mercy. But God can do little with the person who is satisfied with his own judgment of accepting bad as good. God is willing to forgive a person who admits a need for forgiveness. But God can do nothing for one who believes in his heart that he needs no forgiveness because he has done nothing wrong. The tragic attitude of our man in the parable is that he is convinced it wasn't his fault at all. The master's hardness made him do it. God forgives failures, but even God cannot forgive a fool. And the man who stands before God and says he has done no wrong is a fool.

## Act Three

The third act of this tragic story is that when our tragic hero finally is convinced he was wrong and needs forgiveness, it is too late to do anything about it. All his money is taken from him and he is fired from his job. This note of finality is frequently sounded throughout the New Testament. There is a time limit on life and grace. God is a merciful God, but there is an apparent limit to his mercy. The time comes when the day of grace has ended and fools are left in the darkness to cry and gnash their teeth.

So this is the basic drama of the one-talent man. He was wrong and didn't know it. When he was forced to face his wrongness, he wouldn't admit it but blamed it on someone else. And when he finally came to realize that he needed to be forgiven, it was too late. He should be a warning to us all.

## Trust

One more interpretation needs to be added. This is to view the parable as a story of trust. There are just two main characters so far as the basic plot is concerned — the master and the unfaithful servant.

The story begins with an act of trust on behalf of the master. He entrusts his property to his servants. The literary function of the first two servants forms the necessary background for the third servant. They establish the contrast which shows wherein the third servant failed.

The first two servants return the trust their master had in them by trusting him. They put his money to work and earned for him a sizable profit. In the beginning of the story the third man experienced the same trust of the master as the other two men. The third man, however, did not trust his master in return. Rather, he responded to trust with fear. His fear was non-productive and was condemned by the master. The point of the story is that our experience of **being** trusted should engender trust in us.

Hunter believes the parable was directed to the religious leaders of Israel. God had "entrusted them with his Word — his unique revelation of himself and his will in the Law and Prophets — they had fallen down on their trust." What should have been shared with the Gentiles, they had hoarded away. And Hunter concludes, "Such hoarding was tantamount to defrauding God of his own."³ The Jewish leaders were basically afraid of God, and fear cancels out trust.

Now what does this say to us today? First, it points up the necessity of our knowing that we are trusted. So often all we ever hear is that we are to trust in God. But seldom do we hear that God trusts us. This is important because before we can trust, we must know that we are trusted.

A young man was released from prison and was given a job in a grocery store. The owner of the store knew the young man's background but treated him like any other employee. At the end of the week he trusted him to take the money to the bank.

After several years the young man was made assistant manager of the store. Then one morning he came in to discover that the safe had been robbed. He panicked. He told the owner he was going to run away because when the police found out that he had been in prison for safecracking, they would be certain he was guilty. But the store owner said, "Trust me. Everything will be all right. You are innocent and that's the only thing that is important. Stay and prove it." After some very bad days and nights of accusations on the part of the police, the men who robbed the safe were apprehended.

When it was all over the store owner said to the young man, "I'm glad you trusted my advice and didn't break and run." To which the young man replied, "How could I do anything but trust you, for you're the only person in my whole life who ever trusted me.''

We need to hear and to know that we are trusted. Many a young person has gone wrong because he never felt his parents trusted him. Many marriages have been wrecked by jealousy resulting from a lack of trust. And many people fail to serve and trust in God because they have never heard of God's unbending trust in them. Paul says that the three great Christian virtues are faith, hope and love. And it should be added, trust is what holds these three great virtues together. Faith is trusting that what God says in his Word is true. Hope is trusting in the promises God makes. And love is trusting in the Word and the promise that God loves us.

# *11*

# A Carpenter on the Throne

### The Parable of the Sheep and the Goats
### Matthew 25:31-46

This parable is packed with surprises. The great day of judgment comes, and it takes place, not in the courtroom of the law as we would imagine, but in the throne room of the Son of Man. What happens is not a trial where issues are argued and defended; rather is it like the everyday occurrence of a shepherd separating sheep from goats.

Everyone who hears this parable of judgment is surprised. The theologian discovers that what he regards as absolutely essential — the creeds and sound doctrine — are not even mentioned. The moralist is shocked that clean living and temperance play no part in the decision. The liturgist discovers that devotion and ritual prayer receive no attention. The evangelist hears no word about conversion or decision. Rather, the shepherd-judge says that the decisive moments of destiny occurred when a cup of cool water was given to a thirsty man, when food was given to the hungry, when friendship was shared with the lonely, and comfort brought to the sick. Everyone is surprised. The religious discover they are not as good as they thought they were, and the irreligious discover they are not as bad as they had been told they were.

Suddenly structures of ethical standards collapse before the shepherd of surprises. Judgment is a word we have known and used is redefined, and we have to struggle to find a place to take a stand. We are literally knocked off of our feet of faith.

## Judgment

At first in the Old Testament, the idea of judgment was a picture of God ruling on a particular issue or case. It was synonymous with "the good opinion of God." Gradually, as the Jews settled down to claim a home for themselves and were threatened by angry neighbors, the idea of a great day of judgment developed when the righteous would be set on high and their enemies would be revenged. It was called the "Day of the Lord," when the faithful people of God would be rewarded and the hated heathen would be doomed.

During the intertestamental period the idea of a resurrection of the dead was developing, and with it, the idea of a day of universal judgment for all came to be an accepted belief. At first, God as the King of Israel was identified as judge, but gradually the idea developed that God would delegate the judgment of the earth to a Messianic prince who would at the same time establish the Kingdom of God.

This idea becomes firmly entrenched in the statement of the creed where Christ sits "at the right hand of God the Father Almighty. From thence he shall come to judge the quick and the dead."

It is surprising that Jesus in his teaching ministry has so little to say about a final judgment. He does occasionally talk of hell, but even then he never uses judgment as a threat. As Regin Prenter points out, "It is not true that Jesus ever threatened people with hell. He did, however, warn against it."[1] The difference between a threat and a warning is that a warning is a compassionate expression of concern, like a highway sign indicating a dangerous curve. A threat, on the other hand, is a harsh expression of aggression like a doubled-up fist shaken under the nose.

In the Parable of the Sheep and the Goats, Christ issues a warning in love. It is not a prescription but a description. A prescription is something that we must do if we are to achieve a desired end. A description is a picture of the way things are, or will be. Sheep and goats are not made sheep and goats by judgment; they are only identified for what they are. Therefore, judgment reveals what has long been true. The deeds of mercy which the sheep performed were not works of merit but examples and evidences of the fact they were sheep and not goats. Therefore, judgment is not a threat of something to be feared in the future, but a warning that one day all people will be revealed for what they are now.

Wallace[2] points out that judgment does not take place at the last day but now. We are judged each day as we react to our neighbor. No decision is made by the judge on judgment day. It is only then that the announcement is made of the verdict already established by the way we have lived our lives. The last day is not so much Judgment Day as it is **Verdict Day**. Then the true nature of our being will be revealed. This is the surprising truth about judgment: it depends ultimately not on what we do, or fail to do, but on what we are — sheep or goats.

## Sheep and Goats

The picture of a shepherd separating sheep from goats used as a metaphor of judgment is not surprising. It goes back as far as Ezekiel 34:17. Why goats are chosen to represent the unrighteous is not easy to determine. They were sure-footed climbers and rather independent creatures when compared to sheep. They shared an equally important place in the daily economy of people. They could not be fleeced like the sheep, but they did provide rich milk and savory cheese for the table.

It is interesting to speculate that Jesus may have seen in the image of the sheep the faithful disciples who followed him. The image of the sure-footed climbing goats may have suggested to him the ambitious Pharisees as they worked to elevate themselves above the ordinary people of the herd.

### Who Is Being Judged?

One big question facing the interpretation of this parable is who is it that is being judged? The Jews, as we have mentioned above, looked forward to a general judgment of all people which would vindicate them as the chosen people of God and punish their enemies.

Henry B. Swete in his book, *The Parables of the Kingdom*[3], holds that Jesus has judged his servants and his followers in Matthew 25:12. Now he is judging the rest of humankind. It is the judgment of those who have had no opportunity of hearing the word about Jesus as the Christ and Savior of humankind.

John Morey in his book, *The Parables of the Kingdom*[4], believes it is not a judgment of individuals at all but of nations and governments. Here, governments that have been concerned for the social welfare of the people and fed the hungry and clothed the poor will be recognized and rewarded.

The average sermon preached on this text takes the moralistic approach, which is that the parable is a picture of the final day of judgment when the good people will be separated from the bad. The good go to heaven and the bad to hell.

### Inhumanity

No matter who is established as being judged, the surprising fact to those who first heard the parable was that judgment is based on how you treat others. The Jews were certain that membership in the chosen race would be the basis of judgment. The Pharisees were more limited in their view and saw faithful obedience and observation of the Law as the only possible standard of judgment. But the parable points out that the issue is not heritage but humanity. The goats were guilty not of immorality, but of inhumanity. The Pharisees must have been more than surprised; they must have been shocked to discover that on the day of judgment the goats were condemned, not for breaking the needed Law, but for neglecting needy people.

## Relationship to Christ

Perhaps the greatest surprise is that acts of kindness and service are meritorious not in and of themselves, but that in doing them to the needy people you are actually doing them to Jesus. This means that love is no longer just the great commandment, but a personal response and relationship to God. All acts of kindness and service are encounters with the person of the Lord. God does not just observe good deeds and then reward them; he is actually the recipient of the deeds.

The parable thereby personalizes obedience from some cold application of the law and makes of it a warm personal relationship with the Lord.

## Brothers

We have seen that there is no agreement as to who is being judged — the disciples, pagans, all humankind, or the nations of the world. There is also a lack of agreement as to who are the "brothers" or "the least of these my brethren." Hunter,[5] expressing the opinion of most scholars, believes "brethren" to be all humanity that is in need. We will be judged by our acts of compassion to all the poor and afflicted people whose paths have crossed ours.

Fuller[6], on the other hand, believes that "brothers" used in Matthew always means disciples. Therefore, in this parable Jesus is talking to his close followers, attempting to comfort them in the light of the mistreatment they have been receiving

152

from the world. The people of the world will be judged by how they treat those who confess the name of Christ and follow in his ways.

Harvey,[7] in a somewhat similar interpretation, takes the position that "brethren" is a technical name for Christians in the New Testament. Therefore, rewards will be given to those who show kindnesses to the followers of Jesus. These are the Body of Christ in the world, and as people treat them so they treat Christ the Lord.

Findly[8] interprets the term "brethren" as referring to the Jewish people. Jesus, knowing that soon the chosen people of God will be scattered throughout the world and knowing that they will suffer much persecution, tells this parable as a warning to all nations that they will be judged by how they treat "The Wandering Jew."

If scholars like Fuller and Harvey are right and "brethren" means a disciple of Christ, then the parable is a dramatization of the ancient Hebrew Shaliach Principle which is: the acceptance or rejection of an accredited agent involves the rejection or acceptance of the sender. Jesus is therefore pointing out that his followers are his representatives in the world, and at the last judgment all persons will be judged by how they are treated. This would mean that all those sermons which have been preached on this text, calling people within the church to humanitarian service outside the church, have been seriously missing the teaching of the text. The point of the parable would be just the opposite. Rather than a challenge to social action, it is a pastoral word of comfort to Christians that as they are mistreated by the world, they will ultimately be revenged by the judgment of God on an unreceptive world.

### Danger

No matter how we interpret "brethren," this parable should not be used as the key that unlocks the mystery of divine judgment. Nor should we conclude that all we have to do to guarantee our right status on judgment day is to feed the hungry, clothe the naked, and visit the imprisoned. This would lead to an absolute certainty that would undermine the stance of faith.

The danger is that the parable on the surface seems to be so clear and simple. It presents a picture of division between the sheep who serve the Lord in serving the needy ones, and the goats who do not. Judgment, the parable tells us, is not only a mystery but a great surprise. In the parable, the righteous and the unrighteous were both surprised. They were not consciously endeavoring to achieve heaven or avoid hell. "When, Lord?" both the sheep and the goats cry out when faced with their judgment. The righteous were good without being aware of it. The unrighteous ignored the good without being aware of it. The unrighteous ignored the Lord without even knowing it. Therefore, to interpret this parable as an exhortation to serve the Lord through those in need, is to encourage in the minds of the listeners an attitude contrary to the very central thrust of the parable. Lack of awareness is an essential characteristic of true Christian service. For in no other way could surprise be the reaction of those who had done good.

### Spontaneous Goodness

Here is the snag of the parable that catches us all and tears to shreds our neat little moral conclusions drawn from the story of the sheep and the goats. The parable makes us aware of what we are to do unconsciously and spontaneously. It is obvious that the moment we become aware of what we are to do, we cannot do it unconsciously or spontaneously. It is like finding out beforehand about a surprise party given in our honor. There is no way we can forget we haven't heard about it and be genuinely surprised. The parable seems to create an impossible expectation.

## A Holy Habit

However, there is a way that we can consciously move to an action which is unconsciously done. When something is done so often that it becomes a habit, then there is a point where an action is completed without conscious attention to that action. Take driving a car, for example. At first each little movement of hands or feet is a deliberately directed action. We keep our mind on the job, every second seriously concentrating on each and every movement made. After a while the process becomes totally an unconscious process. While we are driving, our minds are free to think of many other things.

Now so it can be with Christian service and moral action. At the beginning, there is a consciousness of the directive that we are to serve others and so serve the Lord. But as such service and good deeds to others become a habit — a life style — it becomes something done without conscious effort. We do good without knowing it.

So Jesus is pointing out in this parable of judgment that the final test is not doing good deeds, but being a good person — being a sheep and not a goat. That is being the type of person for whom service to those in need is the natural expression of his/her life style. Spontaneous service becomes a holy habit.

## A Carpenter on the Throne

The final surprise is perhaps the greatest surprise of all. Jesus places himself upon a throne in the story of this parable and assigns to himself the role of the King who judges the nations of the world. Harvey states, "This represents a greater concentration of attributes in the person of the Son than appears anywhere else in the Gospels."[9] In most instances Christ prefers to take a completely subordinate position to the Father. But here, for a few moments at least, he usurps in our minds the traditional position of God the

Father. In this parable the Son of Man occupies the dramatic center of the judgment scene completely. This suggests to some that this parable may have been the creation of the Early Church rather than an original teaching of Jesus. The Early Church might have felt that the suffering servant image, so common to the Gospels, needed the balance of the kingly emphasis to present the total witness of their experience of Jesus as the Christ.

Many scholars believe that it may have been Matthew's concern with the "law of love" as the great commandment that led him to give Jesus this exclusive and elevated role in the final judgment. Love was the most distinguishing mark of Jesus' teachings, over against the pharisaic tradition. It would be only natural, therefore, and consistent that Matthew, believing love to be the criterion by which we are judged, would demand that the teacher of love be the final judge of those who had succeeded or failed to follow his great commandment of love. Peter Ellis[10] suggests this when he points out that the parable is not so much our Lord's as it is Matthew's expressed compulsion with the law of love.

Whatever the speculation concerning the origin and intent of Christ on the throne of judgment, this surprising image of the parable does stand as a fantastic claim. Christ the peasant, son of a carpenter from Nazareth, is now king, sitting on a royal throne to judge the nations and the people gathered before him. Lowly Jesus born in a stable, penniless in life, executed on a criminal's cross, has now ascended to the royal throne.

Here in the parable is the great note of comfort for us all. The issue is not so much the standard by which we will be judged, but who it is that will be our judge. On that decisive day when we stand before judgment, it is our Lord and Savior who holds our destiny in his hands.

A young man who was not really bad became associated with some hardened criminals. Through them he became involved in a bank robbery. He had only driven the get-away car but he was charged along with the others as guilty of grand theft.

The young man asked his lawyer about his chances, and he answered, "Well, it's like this: there are three possible judges that might try your case. Two are hanging judges, and they will throw the book at you. But the third judge is concerned to rescue young men like yourself from a life of habitual crime. It all depends on whom you get as judge."

The young man spent some restless days and nights going over in his mind what would happen to him because of his foolish fling. Then one morning his lawyer came to him with the news — "You got the right judge. Your chances are good."

So as we face the final judgment, we rejoice, for we have a righteous and merciful judge. The Lamb of God sits on the throne. And that throne is in the shape of a cross, and the crown he wears is one of thorns. And the hand he raises to separate out the sheep bears the marks of nails. What a fantastic surprise! What a grand and glorious surprise! The dreadful day so many have feared is instead a day of great rejoicing. The Good Shepherd has come to claim his sheep.

# Notes

## 1

1. R. H. Charles, *The Apocrypha and Pseudepigrapha of the Old Testament II* (Oxford Press).

## 2

1. Joachim Jeremias, *The Parables of Jesus* (New York, Charles Scribner's Sons, 1955), p. 61.
2. Charles Francis Digby Moule, *The Birth of the New Testament* (New York, Harper and Row, 1962), p. 218.
3. Eta Linnemann, *Jesus of the Parables* (New York, Harper and Row, 1966), p. 115.
4. A. M. Hunter, *The Parables Then and Now* (Philadelphia, Westminister Press, 1971), p. 37.
5. Helmut Thielicke, *The Waiting Father* (New York, Harper and Brothers, 1959), p. 53.
6. A. M. Hunter, op. cit. p. 38.
7. David M. Granskou, *Preaching on the Parables* (Philadelphia, Fortress Press, 1972), p. 65.

## 3

1. C. H. Dodd, *The Parables of the Kingdom* (New York, Charles Scribner's Sons, 1956), p. 147.
2. Joachim Jeremias, *The Parables of Jesus* (New York, Charles Scribner's Sons, 1955), p. 20.
3. Gerald Kennedy, *The Parables* (New York, Harper and Brothers, 1960), pp. 44-52.
4. Emil Brunner, *Sowing and Reaping* (Richmond, John Knox Press, 1965), p. 71.
5. Joachim Jeremias, op. cit. p. 81.
6. David Granskou, *Preaching on the Parables* (Philadelphia, Fortress Press, 1972), pp. 68-71.
7. Gerald Kennedy, op. cit. p. 46.
8. Martin Luther, *Works of Martin Luther, Vol. II.*
9. Ulrich Zwingli, *Selected Works of Zwingli*, ed. by Samuel Macauley Jackson (Philadelphia, University of Pennsylvania Press, 1972), p. 149.
10. A. M. Hunter, *The Parables Then and Now* (Philadelphia, Westminster Press, 1971), p. 48.
11. Ronald S. Wallace, *Many Things in Parables* (New York, Harper and Brothers, 1955), p. 35.
12. C. H. Dodd, op. cit. p. 147.
13. John Calvin, *Institutes of the Christian Religion, Vol. I* (Philadelphia,

Presbyterian Board of Christian Education, 1936), p. 460.

14. Emil Brunner, *Sowing and Reaping* (Richmond, John Knox Press, 1946), p. 73.

**4**

1. A. M. Hunter, *The Parables Then and Now* (Philadelphia, Westminster Press, 1971), p. 78.
2. Eta Linnemann, *Jesus of the Parables* (New York, Harper and Row, 1966), p. 100.
3. *Ibid.* p. 101.
4. William Barclay, *The Gospel of Matthew, Vol. 2* (Philadelphia, Westminster Press, 1958), p. 96.

**5**

1. Joachim Jermias, *The Parables of Jesus* (New York, Charles Scribner's Sons, 1955), p. 177.
2. Eta Linnemann, *Jesus of the Parables* (New York, Harper and Row, 1964), p. 105.
3. Joachim Jeremias, op. cit. p. 145.
4. *Ibid.* p. 147.

**6**

1. Charles W. F. Smith, *The Jesus of the Parables* (Philadelphia, A Pilgrim Press Book from United Church Press, 1975), p. 87.
2. William Oscar Emil Oesterley, *The Gospel Parables in the Light of Their Jewish Background* (London, Society for Promoting Christian Knowledge, 1936), p. 100.
3. C. H. Dodd, *The Parables of the Kingdom* (New York, Charles Scribner's Sons, 1956), p. 122.
4. Joachim Jeremias, *The Parables of Jesus* (New York, Charles Scribner's Sons, 1955), p. 23.
5. *Ibid* p. 36.
6. *Ibid* p. 38.
7. Helmut Thielicke, *The Waiting Father* (New York, Harper and Brothers, 1959), pp. 115-125.
8. Fred H. Lindemann, *The Sermon and the Propers, Vol. II* (St. Louis, Concordia Publishing House, 1958), p. 26.
9. Martin Luther, *Sermons on the Gospels, Vol. I* (Rock Island, IL, Augustana Book Concern, 1871), pp. 280-292.
10. Edmund Stimle, *Are You Looking for God?* (Philadelphia, Muhlenberg Press, 1957), pp. 23-29.

**7**

1. A. M. Hunter, *The Parables Then and Now* (Philadelphia,

Westminster Press, 1971), p. 104.
2. Ronald S. Wallace, *Many Things in Parables* (New York, Harper and Brothers, 1955), p. 164.
3. Dan Otto Via, *The Parables* (Philadelphia, Fortress Press, 1967), p. 136.
4. *Ibid.* p. 137.
5. A. E. Harvey, *The English Bible, Companion to the New Testament* (Oxford University Press, 1971), pp. 178-179.
6. Charles W. F. Smith, *The Jesus of the Parables* (Philadelphia, A Pilgrim Press Book from United Church Press, 1975), p. 132.
7. *Ibid.* p. 134.
8. David Granskou, *Preaching on the Parables* (Philadelphia, Fortress Press, 1972), p. 111.
9. Helmut Thielicke, *The Waiting Father* (New York, Harper and Brothers, 1959), p. 105.

8

1. Alfred Plumer, *The Gospel According to Luke: The International Critical Commentary* (Edinburgh, T. & T. Clark, 1956), p. 362.
2. Kenneth Bailey, *New Perspectives on the Parables* (Pittsburgh, Thesis Cassettes, 1974).
3. Eta Linnemann, *Jesus of the Parables* (New York, Harper and Row, 1964), p. 89.
4. Dietrich Bonhoeffer, *No Rusty Swords* (New York, Harper and Row, 1965).

9

1. A. E. Harvey, *The New English Bible, Companion to the New Testament* (Oxford University Press, 1971), p. 96.
2. A. M. Hunter, *The Parables Then and Now* (Philadelphia, Westminster Press, 1971), p. 101.
3. Charles Francis Digby Moule, *The Birth of the New Testament* (New York, Harper and Row, 1962), p. 101.
4. Eta Linnemann, *Jesus of the Parables* (New York, Harper and Row, 1966), p. 127.
5. Joachim Jeremias, *The Parables of Jesus* (New York, Charles Scribner's Sons, 1955), p. 41.
6. Eta Linnemann, op. cit. p. 125.
7. Ronald S. Wallace, *Many Things in Parables* (New York, Harper and Brothers, 1955), p. 179.
8. Dan Otto Via, *The Parables* (Philadelphia, Fortress Press, 1967), p. 125.
9. *Ibid.* p. 126.
10. Heinz Zahrnt, *The Question of God* (New York, Harcourt, Brace and World, 1966), p. 115.

160

**10**

1. G. E. P. Cox, *The Gospel According to St. Matthew: The Torch Commentary* (London, S. C. M. Press, Ltd., 1952), p. 150.
2. David Granskou, *Preaching on the Parables* (Philadelphia, Fortress Press, 1972), p. 123.
3. A. M. Hunter, *The Parables Then and Now* (Philadelphia, Westminster Press, 1971), p. 97.

**11**

1. Regin Prenter, *Creation and Redemption* (Philadelphia, Fortress Press, 1967), p. 574.
2. Ronald D. Wallace, *Many Things in Parables* (New York, Harper and Brothers, 1955), p. 190.
3. Henry B. Swete, *The Parables of the King* (London, Macmillan and Co., 1920), p. 152.
4. John Morey, *The Parables of the Kingdom* (London, Covenant Publishing Co., 1940), p. 181.
5. A. M. Hunter, *The Parables Then and Now* (Philadelphia, Westminster Press, 1971), p. 117.
6. Reginald H. Fuller, *Preaching the Lectionary: The Word of God for the Church Today* (Collegeville, Minn., Liturgical Press, 1974), p. 280.
7. A. E. Harvey, *The New English Bible: Companion to the New Testament* (Oxford University Press, 1971), p. 100.
8. J. Alexander Findly, *Jesus and the Parables* (London, Epworth Press, 1957), p. 108.
9. A. E. Harvey, op. cit. p. 99.
10. Peter Ellis, *Matthew: His Mind and His Message* (Collegeville, Minn., Liturgical Press, 1974), pp. 93-94.